HMS HERMES

A Pictorial History

Lieutenant Commander Tony Dyson Royal Navy

Foreword by Admiral of the Fleet
Lord Lewin KG, GCB, MVO, DSC

Published by Maritime Books, Lodge Hill, Liskeard,
Cornwall PL14 4EL, and printed and bound in Great
Britain by A. Wheaton and Co. Ltd, Exeter, Devon.

Contents

Foreword

It takes all sorts to make a Navy: Big Ship men and Small Ship men, Submariners and Airy Fairies, and each will stoutly defend his preference as the only life. A Small Ship man myself, when I was told that my next draft was Captain of HMS *Hermes* I thought this will be interesting but not much fun. How wrong I was. My commission of 66–67 turned out to be the happiest and most exciting of my career, before or since, and I am sure that many of those who served in her in her twenty-five year life have a very special affection for 'Happy Hermes'.

Tony Dyson has brilliantly compressed a quarter of a century of ship history into these pages; inevitably his text and the many splendid photographs will evoke in old Hermites other memories of our particular times. He includes Pete Shepherd's somewhat dramatic arrival on the first night deck landing of 1966 but not his remark — "What a hell of a way to arrive" — as he stepped from his slightly bent Sea Vixen. Nor that as he made his long approach on the CCA the ship was chasing a light and variable wind at twenty-four knots towards the far too proximate coast of Dorset, and that it was a toss-up which would happen first, he would hit the deck or we would hit the beach.

At the other end of the commission many of my lot will remember Pete's breathtaking solo areobatic display to celebrate his 4000th flying hour while the ship steamed off the Cocos Islands, and the suitably inscribed coconut that was presented to him afterwards to mark the occasion. I wonder if he has still got it? But these are just a couple of recollections for those of us who were there in 66–67; reading these pages, looking at these pictures, will stir in others their own special memories, some happy, some sad.

It says a great deal for the wartime ship designers and ship builders that *Hermes*, conceived in the days of the Swordfish and Fulmar before the first jet aircraft flew, had the flexibility to adapt to four entirely separate existences; as a Strike Carrier operating Buccaneers and Vixens, as a Commando Carrier when her main armament was 600 Royal Marines, as an Anti-Submarine Carrier, then finally as a Sea King and Harrier Carrier, flagship of a Task Force fighting a war way down on the edge of the Antarctic. For me the last episode had particularly strong *Hermes* connections. Her Captain, Lin Middleton, had commanded the Buccaneer squadron, 809, in 66–67. The Task Force Commander, Admiral Sir John Fieldhouse, had been my Commander. *Hermes*' contribution to that remarkable maritime campaign in the South Atlantic deserves a book to itself, those of us who served in the Old Lady in earlier days were immensely proud of our successors. Alone of all the hard-working postwar strike carriers, she was called upon to fight a war. She ended her career in a blaze of glory and has earned her place in history.

Terence Lewin

1

The tenth HMS Hermes, built at Barrow
1943 to 1959

The story of the tenth HMS *Hermes* began on 12 July 1943, when Mr Bernard Pool, Deputy Director of Naval Contracts, wrote to Vickers Armstrong at Barrow.

> 'I have to request that you will proceed with the construction and completion in all respects of one in number Light Fleet Carrier for His Majesty's Navy.'

This was the birth certificate for HMS *Hermes*, but many twists and changes to the story were to occur before she commissioned and hoisted the White Ensign on 18 November 1959.

In July 1943 the country was still at war. True, there were the first dim gleams of victory, but at sea battle losses demanded shipyards to be kept at full stretch replacing both merchant and military vessels. Also, with an eye to the task after the defeat of Germany and the liberation of Europe there was the enormous task of beating the Japanese forces, sprawled across the Pacific and South East Asia. Looking further than anti-submarine vessels, the Admiralty saw the need for aircraft carriers, to 'carry the war to the enemy.' By 1 October 1943 the drawings for the new light fleet carrier of 22,000 tons, to be called the *Elephant*, had been completed by the Barrow draughtsmen, and by November the first offsets were laid in the mould loft. The ship had left the drawing board.

Eight ships of the class were ordered; the others being *Centaur, Albion, Bulwark, Monmouth, Polyphemus, Arrogant,* and *Hermes*. The first three were soon under construction, and the keel of *Elephant* was laid down on 21 June 1944. By 1945 work was going ahead fast. The demands of the British Pacific and East Indies Fleet were throwing a severe strain on the Fleet Air Arm, and every available fleet carrier in commission was already in the Far East. Still more carriers were urgently needed if our Pacific Fleet was to continue to play a significant role alongside the task forces of the US Navy. There was the need to provide air cover for the eventual landings on the Japanese mainland, and subsequent operations ashore which were forecast to place even greater strain on carriers of both navies.

Then came the atom bomb, and, with the mushroom clouds rising over Hiroshima and Nagasaki, a sudden end to the Second World War. With the coming of peace, came the need to rationalise a peacetime fleet. All work on the *Elephant* was halted, although this was a better fate than four of the class suffered, as the *Polyphemus, Monmouth, Arrogant* and *Hermes* were cancelled. With the original *Hermes* now cancelled, the Admiralty decided to perpetuate a name that had close connections with the birth of the Fleet Air Arm. Accordingly, the *Elephant* was renamed *Hermes* and became the tenth ship since 1796 to bear the name in the Royal Navy.

The outlook for the ship was not good. The only warships being completed were those whose construction was well advanced and which had, in most cases, been launched. On the date when work stopped on the *Hermes* the shell was up to middle deck level and the main internal bulkheads had been completed. For the next three years little other than maintenance work was done, including continuously coating the steelwork with oil.

But there was at that time a great need for merchant shipping, to replace wartime losses, and every available building berth was needed. So, in 1949, it was decided to go ahead and complete the ship up to the launching stage, in order to clear the slip. On 16 February 1953 she was launched by Lady Clemantine (then Mrs Winston) Churchill. By the middle of 1953 all work had again virtually stopped. In the press and elsewhere questions were raised: would she ever be completed? Then came another significant letter from the Admiralty: '. . . Since these ships were designed, numerous additions have been made as the result of new staff requirements, the lessons of the war, and the partial return to peacetime amenities'.

By now the angled deck, the steam catapult and the mirror deck landing aid had arrived. When at last plans were received from the Admiralty it was clear that it was not just a case of making modifications to the existing plans, but more that a new ship was to be built within the confines of the original hull as laid down.

With stand-off bombs and guided missiles coming into service, the need for a multitude of close and medium range armaments had gone. The 4.5 inch guns and all but ten of the 40 mm Bofors, together with the 20 mm Oerlikons were removed. Magazine stowage and ammunition supply hoists all had to be removed or modified. The fitting of the steam catapults at the forward end of the flight deck caused many headaches — to allow for the tremendous increase in thrust demanded, and the heavier weight of new aircraft, the ship's structure had to be drastically strengthened. New and heavier longitudinal bulkheads supporting the catapult troughs and machinery were fitted, and additional stiffening was required not only for the gallery deck, but several below as well. To place the deck edge lift outside the hull required the strengthening of surrounding areas of shell, hangar deck plating and hangar bulkheads to support the overhanging load. Consequently it was decided to build the lift supports and other adjacent structure of special steel. The 'island' structure was completely redesigned and, in place of the foremast, provision was made for a new 984 Comprehensive Display System Radar Antenna, weighing 28 tons.

New air to air weapons such as the 'Firestreak' missile meant that much more space was demanded for air weapon stowage, and newer and heavier aircraft meant strengthening both flight and hangar decks and widening and strengthening the after centre line lift. Another major change was to allow accommodation and domestic spaces and fittings for the new scheme of complement, which had increased significantly to a crew of over 1,200 men plus the air group.

To meet the new demands of the nuclear warfare era a remote control system for engine and boiler room was designed and built. Perhaps nothing out of the ordinary for ships built and introduced into service in the 80s, but certainly revolutionary and testing for the 50s. A separate supply of air for ship and boilers was constructed, and 'pre-wetting' equipment fitted to all exposed decks. Two separate fuel systems for jet and piston engined aircraft (Avcat and Avgas) were provided, necessitating new and larger fuel stowage space, pumps and fuel lines; a new liquid oxygen plant was fitted, a mirror landing aid on a new sponson, and an angled flight deck. Crew accommodation was completely updated, and was the most modern fitted at its time, and a whole host of other modifications were introduced. But despite all these complications, the builders gave Admiral Sir Peter Reid KCB CVO, then Controller of the Navy, an assurance in 1957 that *Hermes* would be complete by the end of October 1959. At times Barrow had over two thousand men working on the ship, to say nothing of sub-contractors, but true to their word, HMS *Hermes* sailed from Barrow for the last time on 1 November 1959.

In May 1959 *Hermes* had sailed from Barrow to Southampton, where she docked down in the King George V Dry Dock. After essential maintenance prior to acceptance she sailed for contractor's sea trials before returning to Barrow for final fitting out. Some embarrassment had been experienced when it had been found that *Hermes* was too large to squeeze out of the Buccleuch basin without removing the bilge keels, and even after their removal the railway bridge had to be tipped up beyond its normal maximum angle to allow safe clearance to the island superstructure. Despite British Rail's and the shipbuilder's mutual anxieties, eventual safe passage was achieved with a clearance of about eight to nine inches, and the ship sailed to Southampton on 1 November 1959. Bilge keels replaced and angled flight deck completed, on 17 November *Hermes* sailed down Southampton Water wearing the Red Ensign for the last time. The next morning, after final full power trials, a simple but impressive ceremony was held on the flight deck, at which the acceptance documents were signed by Captain D S Tibbets DSC Royal Navy, *Hermes'* first commanding officer, on behalf of the Admiralty, and Mr L Redshaw, General Manager of Vickers-Armstrong (Shipbuilders). As the ship's future flight from 849 NAS flew by, the Red Ensign was lowered, the bugle sounded, the Royal Marine Guard presented arms and the White Ensign was hoisted. The tenth *Hermes* was now HMS . . .

Right HMS Hermes is launched at Barrow on 16 February 1953 by Lady Clemantine (then Mrs Winston) Churchill

10

Above Will she make it? **Hermes** *approaches Buccleuch Basin Bridge on her final departure from Barrow, 30 October 1959.*

Right Yes, just! With eight to nine inches to spare, **Hermes** *is eased through.*

Facing, above Ship's Heeling Trials, and (below left) Wardroom Heeling Trials.

Facing, below right The Controller, Admiral Sir Peter Reid KCB CVO inspects the ship's company at Barrow before looking over **HMS Hermes** *on 20 February 1959. Captain (later Sir) D S Tibbets, the first commanding officer, is on the admiral's left.*

Above *Hermes* sails from Barrow

Left *Captain D S Tibbets, first commanding officer, accepts* **HMS Hermes** *on behalf of the Admiralty from Mr L Redshaw, General Manager of Vickers-Armstrong (shipbuilders) on 18 November 1959.*

Facing *HMS Hermes enters Portsmouth, her base port, for the first time.*

12

2

First Commission
1959 to 1961

Three hours after the acceptance ceremony HMS *Hermes* berthed at Pitch House Jetty, HM Dockyard Portsmouth. By a happy coincidence, the Sea Lords of the Admiralty and most of the Commanders-in-Chief of the various stations of the Royal Navy happened to be holding a meeting on board HMS *Tyne* at Portsmouth that day, and were able to form a most distinguished audience to see the Navy's newest ship berth at her base port for the first time.

One week later, on 25 November 1959, the ship commissioned at Portsmouth. Captain Tibbets read out the Commissioning Warrant to 3,000 ship's company, families and guests gathered in the hangar. Among those who attended were several survivors of the sinking of the previous *Hermes* in 1942, including Admiral Sir Leonard Durnford-Slater, (C-in-C Nore), and Judge Block, who had been the old carrier's Executive Officer.

The following day, before dawn, the ship left Portsmouth for her first real voyage, a brief shake-down cruise to Gibraltar. This proved to be an aptly named trip, as the ship was greeted on arrival by the Vendevale, (a form of gale, not a civic official), which was the worst for twenty-five years. Harbour craft sunk at their moorings, catamarans danced fandangos, and the liner *Braemar Castle* went for a run ashore in La Linea, without a pass! An Avgas lighter bouncing around the harbour caused some anxious moments, and although the Vendevale died down, the ship was chased back to Portsmouth by a gale which reached storm force 15 at its centre!

Much of the following period, until aircraft were embarked in July 1960, was spent at Portsmouth, testing and tuning equipment, especially the catapults. Two huge trolley-like dead loads, nick-named Effie and Lucy, and painted bright yellow, became familiar sights being hurled over the bows; then being recovered — to do it all over again. On 10 May 1960 a foretaste of things to come was experienced, when a Seahawk of 700 Squadron became the first jet aircraft to land on HMS *Hermes*. Flying trials continued for three weeks, until the first Families Day at sea was held on 24 May, with hundreds of the ship's company's

relatives joining by paddle-tug at Spithead. Trials were over, and the ship embarked her aircraft and sailed for the Mediterranean. On board were 804 NAS with the new Scimitar aircraft, a single-seat strike-fighter; 890 NAS with de Havilland Sea Vixen FAW Mark 1 aircraft; 849 NAS 'C' Flight with Fairey Gannet Airborne Early Warning Mark 3 aircraft; and 814 NAS, who had flown the Swordfish from the ninth *Hermes* during the Second World War, but who were now equipped with eight Westland Whirlwind helicopters. With a full complement of 189 officers and 1,643 ratings, and all aircraft safely embarked, the ship arrived in Gibraltar on 9 July to begin the work-up in the Med. In August Exercise Royal Flush III with the USS *Forrestal* and HMS *Ark Royal* as the 'enemy' gave an opportunity to show off the new 984 Radar/Central Display System, before visiting Algiers. Despite unrest there at the time, the French population put themselves out to ensure all on board had a most enjoyable visit. The visit was followed by the ship's first Operational Readiness Inspection (ORI) by the Flag Officer Aircraft Carriers (FOAC), to see if the work-up had brought the ship up to the standard required. Apparently it had, as, after a thorough going-over, *Hermes* was allowed to head back for England — and blue uniforms again.

Having left the Mediterranean, *Hermes* followed the rain clouds to Falmouth, where 814 Squadron were able to visit their home base at Culdrose. The ship however, ruthlessly avoiding Portsmouth for the first of many such occasions, steamed north to Rosyth and participated in a major air defence exercise code-named 'Swordthrust', which tested the Vixens to the limit; 81 sorties were flown, during which 76 day and 26 night interceptions against determined American opposition were successfully prosecuted. The ship returned to Greenock, and all aboard felt like relaxing; the Scottish climate felt differently about it all however, and introduced the ship to weather — a storm at anchor — which made it impossible to run boats, another experience *Hermes* would get to 'appreciate' over the years. Next, via the anti-submarine exercise 'Rumtub', the ship returned to Portsmouth, but only for three weeks, before she set off for the Far East on 7 November 1960.

After live Firestreak firings at RAE Aberporth for each Vixen pilot, and a Gibraltar docking for ship's bottom painting, *Hermes* transited the Suez Canal on 6 December 1960. A brief stop was made at Aden, with Christmas being spent in Columbo and New Year in Singapore. Many of the ship's company made their first acquaintance with HMS *Terror*'s swimming pool and tropical flood-lit sports fixtures, and Sembawang village. If they found this an experience, they completed the process of growing up at the ship's next port of call – the vast American base of Subic Bay in the Philippines. Counted out at all times through a turn-stile type barrier to the nearby village of Olongapo made for a 'run ashore' that, once experienced, was never forgotten!

The deployment continued with a ten day visit to Hong Kong, representing the furthest point from home, before returning to Singapore and eventually sailing for home on 18 February 1961. First, however, came Exercise Jet 61, where ships from Australia, Ceylon, India, Pakistan, New Zealand and Great Britain assembled off Trincomalee. A particularly poignant moment came for *Hermes* when, on 10 March, a service was held on the flight deck as the ship passed over the spot where the ninth *Hermes* was sunk by Japanese bombers off the coast of Ceylon. Off Aden the ship was relieved by HMS *Victorious* after a last 'rabbit-run' (shopping expedition) in the port. A rapid transit of the Suez Canal was followed by a seven day visit to Malta and a four day visit to Naples. After a very short call at Gibraltar, *Hermes* reached Portsmouth on 19 April, having steamed 33,300 miles in 173 days away from England, or an average of 192 miles a day. On the jetty were hundreds of friends and relatives; the Far East cruise was over, and well-earned leave was taken during April and May 1961.

After five weeks' leave the ship sailed to re-embark her squadrons. They had meanwhile been working hard, preparing for participation in the Paris Air Show and the (then) annual 'Shopwindow' exercise. The Paris Air Show posed many problems of timing and planning, but all went smoothly and useful experience was gained for forthcoming participation at the Farnborough Air Show. 'Shopwindow' took the ship to sea from Spithead each day for a week, with visitors ranging from sea cadets to Major Generals, journalists and civilians; all came to see a variety of evolutions carried out by *Hermes*, three frigates and a submarine. One spectacular, unrehearsed and unwanted incident occurred when a Sea Vixen's wing tank burst into flames on launch. Several flight deck personnel were scorched, but the incident was less serious than first feared, and the pilot managed to land the aircraft safely.

A further round of firings, exercises and flying exercises followed before return to Portsmouth. But when the ship sailed next, on 3 June 1961, it was for an eagerly-anticipated trip to the eastern seaboard of North America, to include visits to Norfolk, Boston and Halifax, Nova Scotia, via various exercises. All on board thought this an excellent way to finish the commission, but it was not to be. 'Sabre-waving' by Kassem over Kuwait saw the British government withdrawing ships from Exercises Riptide and Maple Royal off the eastern USA. HMS *Centaur* sailed from Gibraltar through the Canal to wait off Aden, while *Hermes* waited at Gibraltar. The lessening of tension enabled the ship to return home in late July, but the States trip had been lost forever. . . .

To help make up for the disappointment on board at the amended programme, a final short-notice visit was arranged abroad. As more recent *Hermes* ship's company will understand, this had to be Oslo, capital city of Norway. The visit was marred by the tragic crash of a Viking aircraft, carrying a party of British schoolboys, at Stavanger. The accident was deeply felt by the host nation. The ship was honoured by a visit from King Haakon, and a number of personnel were invited to dine at his palace. After Oslo, it was full speed again back to Portsmouth, and off to Lyme Bay for the Buccaneer flying trials. These seemed to be progressing most satisfactorily, with most of the flying programme completed, until one aircraft crashed into the sea on launch, with the loss of both crew members. The trials were thus tragically curtailed, but the ship had to move on to the next item on the programme, which was the Farnborough Air display.

Hermes' Squadrons 804, 890 and 849 'C' Flight took part each day in a combined display with 800 and 899 Squadrons. The whole week was felt to be a great success, particularly when on the first day all military aircraft, other than those from the Royal Navy, were grounded due to bad weather, and the ship and shore squadrons saved the day. On the Saturday of the show the BBC carried a live broadcast from the ship, showing the Air Group taking off for the show, and being recovered afterwards. A BBC request to the pilot to keep within line of sight and within 15 miles of St Catherine's Point, for broadcasting clarity, plus a 20 aircraft launch, is reputed to have been an interesting experience, especially when the first Scimitar's jet efflux distorted the starboard catapult 'Jet Blast Deflector', which could not be lowered in consequence; all remaining aircraft had to launch off the port catapult. The aircraft made Farnborough however with seconds to spare, and all went well. Afterwards the ship anchored, to dine out Captain Tibbets in the wardroom on one of his last nights at sea in the Royal Navy. Farnborough finished on Sunday 10 September, the squadrons flying straight to their parent air stations ashore, and on

Monday 11 September 1961 *Hermes* entered Portsmouth for her first refit.

Thereafter, while the condition of the ship could be imagined (but preferably not experienced) life did occasionally have its brighter side. One such instance came on the day Billy Smart's Circus visited the ship, and gave a splendid show in the hangar, especially remembered for the elephant who went up the after lift to pull on the wires, but who resolved all questions as to the regularity of an elephant's habits, to the dismay of the hangar cleaning party!

In late November 1961, still firmly in refit, Captain Tibbets handed over command to Captain (later Admiral Sir) W D O'Brien.

The very first aircraft recovery on board. A COD Gannet lands on **HMS Hermes** *April 1960.*

The first jet aircraft recovery. A Seahawk of 700 Squadron lands, 10th May 1960.

Facing **HMS Hermes**, *at speed, aircraft ranged; First Commission 1959–1961.*

The first Scimitar to use the steam catapult. Flight deck crew check the strop before launch.

Sea Vixen queue up to use the port catapult. Note the raised jet blast deflector protecting the second aircraft and the 'H' on the tail indicating the aircraft is from **Hermes**.

Facing *After work up and exercises in the Mediterranean,* **Hermes** *enters Algiers August 1960. The ship's company line the decks in tropical white uniform for Procedure 'Alpha'. All aircraft are ranged on deck.*

Left *Hermes' first transit of the Suez Canal, 6 December 1960*

Centre *The captain visits the mess decks, Christmas day in Colombo 1960*

Below *Rough weather between Singapore and Subic, January 1961*

Hermes enters Hong Kong for the first time. Note the reduced number of aircraft — the remainder had disembarked to RAF Kai Tak. Their flying exploits ashore included 'sonic bangs' over Kowloon, to the embarrassment of the ship.

Below *Crossing the line: Neptune's court leaving the forward lift*

Below left *March 1961 — **Hermes** enters Aden, homeward bound.*

Below right *Comedy caption from the ship's Photographic Department at Naples, April 1961*

Bottom *Fashions may have changed, but the occasions haven't. Eager families wait patiently for the brows on the ship's homecoming to Portsmouth 19 April 1961, after six months in the Far East.*

A dramatic sequence of pictures taken during 'Shopwindow', June 1961. A Sea Vixen's wing tank bursts into flame on launch. Several flight deck personnel were scorched, but otherwise the accident was less serious than first feared. The aircraft and pilot recovered ashore successfully.

*Elephants from Billy Smart's circus board **Hermes**, September 1961.*

Below *Naval carrier power 1960: HM ships **Victorious** (nearest camera), **Ark Royal** and **Hermes** at sea for Exercise Swordthrust*

3

Second Commission
1962 to 1964

After a cold and dreary winter refitting in Portsmouth dockyard, 'D' lock was flooded on 9 March 1962 and *Hermes* was afloat again. She was towed to Middle Slip Jetty and completed her refit by storing ship, carrying out arrester and catapult gear trials, embarking anchor and cables and those 1,001 last-minute jobs. Basin trials were commenced in April 1962, when the barber's shop also re-opened! The refit ended on Good Friday, an aptly-named day on this occasion for the ship's company. On 24 April 1962 the ship recommissioned.

After sea trials the ship's air squadrons embarked. 803 NAS with their Scimitars replaced 804 Squadron; 892 NAS with their Sea Vixens replaced 890 Squadron; 'C' Flight AEW Gannets of 849 were replaced by 'B' Flight — and 814 had re-equipped with Wessex helicopters. At the end of May the ship sailed for the Mediterranean.

Despite forebodings about weather in the Bay of Biscay, passage south was in warm sunshine and light winds. The quick run ashore at Gibraltar was the first 'foreign' run for many. Admiral's Divisions followed — the principal sufferers being the Chinese laundry-men, with a huge pile of whites being put in at the last moment. After Gibraltar real work started, with RAS's, followed by day and night flying off Sardinia, and then in the Malta Exercise Areas. Eventually the arrester gear started to play up and the ship operated with an ever-diminishing number of wires before entering Grand Harbour Malta. The squadrons dis-embarked for RNAS Hal Far, as the ship secured alongside Parlatorio Wharf for a Self Maintenance Period. The contrast between an agreeably hot sun ashore, and unpleasant sticky conditions on board soon became familiar. The ship then sailed for the North African coast and the Al Adem bombing range. The submarine *Tiptoe* joined for exercises with 814. Intensive flying finished with a long-range strike on El Adem, in-flight re-fuelling being used on both legs of the strike.

The ship then paid an official visit to Beirut, where she was enthusiastically received, with an extensive programme of hospitality. The St George's Club threw open its portals to all ranks, and *Hermes* responded splendidly by drinking the club out of beer for the first time in its history!

Hermes was lucky to visit such a remarkable city, then a cosmopolitan mixture of cultures, Armenian, Turkish, French and Arabic; she saw modern blocks of offices and flats, markets and shops, before the devastation of the 1984 Civil War.

Intensive flying followed off Cyprus, Crete and Malta, including an Operational Readiness Inspection, before returning to Gibraltar for maintenance. Lieutenant Tristram (803 NAS) received the Queen's Commendation for Valuable Service in the Air at this time. His own colourful account of the incident is given later in the chapter.

Hermes left Gibraltar in company with *Centaur* and an imposing number of escorts to meet the American and French force comprising the Atlantic Strike Fleet. Looking forward to some cool Atlantic weather, the ship had the lot — fog, low cloud, high winds and rain! The exercise however was a success. Towards the end cross-operations were undertaken with aircraft from USS *Forrestal* and *Enterprise*, and concluded with a wash-up at Lisbon. Further exercises followed with *Centaur* and *Clemenceau*, before a visit to Palma — which many regarded as the holiday high-spot of the cruise.

The ship returned from the Mediterranean in October 1962 for maintenance. One particular in-cident en route for home will however be remembered by many, and this was when the after centre line lift became stuck in the lowered position, while most of the aircraft on board were airborne. Happily, disaster was averted before fuel states became critical, when it was discovered that the only fault was that an optimist had driven all the flight deck tractors on to the lift, and was blissfully trying to make the lift carry twice the capacity for which it was designed!

In November, a 20-year Anniversary Dinner to commemorate the Taranto Raid was held in the hangar. Hosted by Flag Officer Aircraft Carriers, the First Sea Lord (Admiral of the Fleet Sir Caspar John) was guest of honour. Out to sea again, the ship carried out what is believed to be the last launch of a Swordfish aircraft from a carrier, before making her way east of Suez for a further Christmas away from home, this time at Singapore. En route, with the aircraft flown off, there was the amusing spectacle of a pre-wetting trial, with an engineering officer prancing fairy-like amongst the fountains on the flightdeck, as he checked blockages.

After Christmas, passage to Subic Bay preceded busy cross-decking operations with the USS *Ranger*, providing grandstand views of roller landings by the USN aircraft on *Hermes*, whose deck appeared terrifyingly small to the Americans and strengthened their conviction that the British were 'nice guys but nuts'. For the Fleet Air Arm's part, the suggestions for landing on the much larger USS *Ranger* varied from 'formation landings' to 'not bothering to put our hooks down'. Passage north to Hong Kong included working with Commonwealth destroyers. Chinese New Year in Hong Kong (where else?), was followed by an exercise where the ship was honoured by the presence of HRH the Duke of Kent, before returning to Hong Kong for a Self Maintenance Period.

A 'show of strength' by the Air Group followed, over Labuan and Brunei. It was heard later that after the flypast, Labuan had to broadcast to local tribesmen that the aircraft had been 'friendly', and that it would be safe to return from the hills. Excitement on the flight deck was maintained during the exercise which followed as occasional 'hang-ups' (malfunctions on firing) were launched across the flight deck after landing. A live 2-inch rocket skidding across the deck tends to keep everyone alert! At last, back to Singapore and a docking period, with the pleasant prospect of living ashore again for a few weeks. Aircraft were launched to fly to temporary shore-side homes, 803 Squadron Scimitars for Butterworth and the Royal Australian Air Force, while 892 Squadron Vixens and 849 'B' Flight Gannets went to Tengah and Seletar to live with the RAF. Before finally landing, however, they joined with the RAF for a grand flypast over the island. Thus depleted, *Hermes* entered harbour with the feeling that she had passed another milestone in the commission.

Then began a witchhunt for cockroaches, the noise of wind-hammers, the haybox meals and all the other things associated with a docking. Engineers emerged from the bowels of the ship and, with dockyard assistance, fitted a spare propellor in place of one which, it was discovered, had a piece missing. The spare had three blades instead of four, but the ship was assured that this wouldn't make any difference. Everywhere in the ship there seemed to be something being done. The bottom was painted, the sides were painted, and the flight deck became a clean grey carpet. After frantic activity, both ashore and on board, the ship undocked, and concluded the period

with a Scimitar making a successful approach and landing under the positive control of the driver of a floating crane! 814 Squadron embarked on HMAS *Melbourne* for the duration of the coming exercise, but very soon the Vixens, Scimitars and Gannets returned. A post-docking RAS was done in good time, followed by practice flying before the major exercise, Sea Serpent. On its conclusion, all aircraft recovered and parked on the flight deck. While peacefully making way towards Manila for the exercise critique and press conference, the ship's jumbo crane broke loose and tried to push one of the Vixens over the side. Fortunately, the attempt was unsuccessful, but it took some time to separate the combatants! *Hermes* eventually anchored in Manila Bay with a SEATO fleet of 57 ships, proud to learn that, in one year, the ship had flown more sorties than during the whole of the previous commission.

The ship's second visit to Hong Kong on this deployment coincided with a heat wave, with 'highest temperature ever recorded' being reached on several successive days, coupled with a serious water shortage. The ship was able to assist by supplying some fresh water ashore.

At the end of May 1963 *Hermes* sailed for Japan, which was to be the highlight of the cruise. Sadly, a major catapult defect was discovered, and all the ship's company saw of Japan was its misty coastline. The ship glumly returned to Singapore, the jet aircraft had to be disembarked ignominiously by road at dead of night, and the addition of a starboard shaft defect led to ten hot days in dock before returning to action at the end of June. The opportunity was taken to replace the ship's own propellor, which reduced vibration at speed. A last frenzied bout of shopping followed, with the fo'c's'le resembling a bazaar.

During the next flying period one Wessex went berserk with ground resonance, and provided the merriest flight deck yet seen in the Far East, with holes in Vixens caused by well-aimed rotor blades. Luckily no one was hurt. Realistic opposition was provided for HMS *Ark Royal*'s Operational Readiness Inspection, after which the ships met off Langkawi for a banyan day.

This period also saw an unusual helicopter operation. Electrical wizards had decided that the Tacan 'dustbin' must be removed from the masthead for repairs. A Wessex had first crack at this lift, but unfortunately somebody neglected to inform the pilot that there were still two bolts to be undone. The ensuing attempts to pull the mast out of the deck or the ship from the sea were interesting, but ruined the winch, so the SAR chopper had a go. Having learnt from big brother's mistake, the lift was immediately successful, though a little hair-raising to the electrical officer concerned. The re-installation went more smoothly a few days later, and it was a pity that such enterprise should prove fruitless, as the beacon still refused to work.

Following replenishment, *Hermes* set off for Gan and Mombasa, crossing the line on 14 July 1963 to suitable celebration. A period at anchor at Mombasa allowed parties to exped in the National Game Park and climb Mount Kilimanjaro. As the ship headed back to sea, everyone looked fitter and more rested after this spell in a cooler climate. Only a few hours short of arrival at Suez however, instructions were received to wait, until relieved by *Victorious*, before transiting the Canal. This delayed the ship for ten days, but eventually relief was effected, and the ship headed home to be reunited with families in Portsmouth.

After a short spell in, it was time to return to sea, to rehearse for a VIP onslaught in 'Unison'. On the last day before the exercise, the Mirror Control Officer was blown over the side by the jet from a taxiing Vixen. He survived the impact with the water and was chagrined to hear coming from his radio as he struggled to remain afloat, a voice saying 'He must be alright, he's swimming'! Perhaps it is as well his transmitter wasn't working! He was hauled out by the SAR chopper team and deposited on deck, somewhat dazed and full of sea water, but otherwise unhurt. It was remarked that, for the big day, a springboard should be provided for him, as his take-off was rather ragged! His reply is not recorded. On the following day Exercise Unison however went successfully,

with some 120 very senior officers and VIP civilians of Commonwealth Defence Forces arriving by Belvederes amidst wind and rain. All — except the very famous — rapidly became anonymous behind foul weather clothing.

Proceeding via Portsmouth (for a change) the ship returned to the Mediterranean for a month, including an exercise best remembered for the runaway Scimitar. Rearing up over its blocks it charged across the flight deck and fiercely attacked an 892 Squadron Vixen. The result was declared a double technical knockout, and an expensive one at that. A five day visit to Barcelona was paid before returning to Portsmouth at the end of October 1963, having finally said goodbye to 892 and 849 'B', who were to join *Centaur* in December.

After Christmas, *Hermes* left Portsmouth for the last time in the second commission and participated in Exercise Phoenix, albeit with 'borrowed' squadrons. On completion 'Boffins' were embarked for initial deck landing trials of the Mk 2 Sea Vixen, and final trials of the Mk 1 Buccaneer. Then in company with members of the Royal Corps of Transport, who had showed much hospitality to the ship throughout the commission, the ship went ice-breaking in Copenhagen, literally. A fast passage was then made to Devonport, for a rapid de-ammunitioning and destoring, and most of the ship's company were drafted. As they left, the dockyard moved in to change the face of HMS *Hermes*, in a refit which was to last until 1966.

HMS Hermes refitting in 'D' lock, Portsmouth Dockyard, winter 1961/2

9 March 1962 — 'the Dock was flooded'

Left and below *Catapult trials alongside Middle Slip Jetty March/April 1962*

Entering Grand Harbour Malta, July 1962

LIEUT TRISTRAM'S Birdstrike Story
***Left** 'Everything blows up in face'; **Right** The 'chicken' afterwards*

Returning from strike in Crete — late for Charlie (as usual) — increased speed — look to see if wingman OK — he is — look ahead again — Good Lord! Chicken right outside front window! — about to climb — too late — bang! everything blows up in face — convinced am dead — open eyes and see nothing but red — obviously not in heaven! — realise am still alive but decide I am about to croak — tell No 2 (Sub Lieut Bosworth) my troubles — he talks me back to ship — can now see a little and decide to attempt a landing — after all Scimitars very expensive — am talked down to deck but still blind as a bat — then at last moment see a white line on port side of deck — land beside it narrowly avoiding removing the Mirror Control Officer's left ear — taxi into Fly One — step out of cockpit — ground crew take one look and go for tot.

Right and below
*Believed to be the
last free take off
of an armed
Swordfish aircraft
— from* **HMS
Hermes** *in
November 1962*

30

Prewetting trials — believed to be east of Suez, November 1962. Note the scantily clad engineers 'prancing among the fountains' as they check the system.

*In company with RFA's **Reliant** and **Resurgent** during 1962/3 Far East deployment*

31

Sea Vixens from 892 Squadron and Scimitars from 803 Squadron fly past off Brunei, February 1963.

High and dry in Singapore for the Docking Period, April 1963

'It took some time to separate the enemies'... The ship's jumbo crane, after breaking loose, assaults a harmless parked Sea Vixen.

'The merriest flight deck yet seen in the Far East'... a very sorry-looking Wessex of 814 Squadron after a particularly violent bout of ground resonance.

Overleaf Hermes' second visit to Hong Kong, Second Commission, May 1963. Note **HMS Lion** berthed astern, and a somewhat different scene to that found in the area today!

Facing, above left *The forrard stump during a RAS(S) (Replenishment at Sea, Solids)*

Facing, above right *'We have lift-off'... At the second attempt, the SAR helo achieves the removal of the Tacon aerial, after the removal of the bolts which frustrated the first attempt!*

Facing, below *The end of* **HMS Ark Royal***'s Operational Readiness Inspection (ORI), as she meets up with* **Hermes** *off Langkawi Island, Malacca Straits, June 1963.*

Top left *'A last frenzied round of shopping'... The transformation on the fo'c's'le, as the ship's company haggle for their bargains when buying last-minute presents at Singapore Naval Base, before heading homeward — June 1963.*

Top right *One day bus tour to Tsavo National Park proved most popular with the ship's company during the Mombasa visit, July 1963.*

Above *Crossing the line ceremony 14 July 1963:* **left** *Captain O'Brien takes his medicine like a man;* **right** *CDR (Air) wasn't easily persuaded.*

Left *July 1963 — during the visit to Mombasa, an intrepid group of mountaineers set off to climb Mount Kilimanjaro, 19,340 feet high. The snow-capped peak greets them in the picture, a five-day walk — but they made it.*

Make and Mend Routine off Aden, July 1963. Ship's company relax on the flight deck. A Gannet tailplane provides some shade.

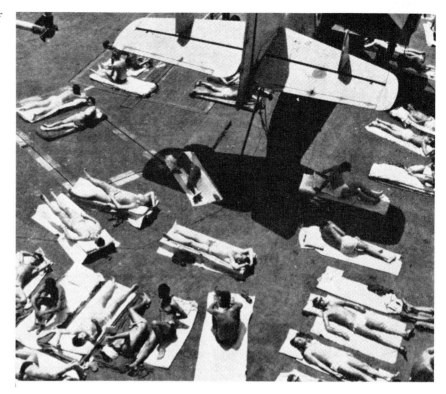

Relieved at last! **Victorious** *arrives to relieve* **Hermes** *as the station carrier East of Suez, July 1963.*

Facing, above *A swift Canal transit en route for home, August 1963*

Facing, below *Home again, to be . . . 'reunited with our families . . . on the jetty'.*

Exercise 'Unison', September 1963:
Hermes *is honoured by the presence of Admiral of the Fleet Lord Louis Mountbatten, arriving by RAF Belvedere helicopter.*

Left *An expensive 'technical knockout': a runaway Scimitar attacks an 892 NAS Sea Vixen with more than mind-bending results;* **right** *A routine Scimitar recovery, sinking to catch arrester wires . . . but possibly too fast a rate of descent?*

Above After a 'bounce' over the arrester wires, the 803 NAS Scimitar takes the barrier . . .

. . . which makes a mess of the aircraft, but stops it!

43

*An 892 NAS Vixen about to be recovered, with **Hermes** making 'best speed' to assist.*

Below *A superb sunset launch of a Vixen — Far East, 1963*

Some things never change: children's parties; **above** *Shanghai, 9th* **Hermes** *1926;* **below** *Barcelona, 10th* **Hermes** *October 1963*

Above Divisions at Sea, back in 'blues', 1963

Shivering at Copenhagen, 'ice breaking' even — on the last run ashore of the Second Commission, February 1964.

4

Third Commission
1966 to 1968

Captain (later Admiral Sir) W D O'Brien DSC left HMS *Hermes* on 5 March 1964, shortly after she entered refit. During the next two years, ten million pounds was spent on the ship. Work included the removal of all guns: their replacement with Seacat surface-to-air missiles made *Hermes* the Fleet's first 'all missile' ship. A longer and more powerful catapult was fitted to operate the Buccaneer Mk 2 and Sea Vixen Mk 2 aircraft, 05 deck was added to the island and Flyco replaced. Full air conditioning was fitted. On 3 February 1966, Captain (later Admiral of the Fleet Lord) T T Lewin MVO DSC assumed command, and on 28 March the ship recommissioned. The 'teeth' of the ship were provided by a squadron new to *Hermes*, 809 NAS, equipped with six of the new Buccaneer Mk 2 aircraft; 892 NAS returned, but with 11 new Vixen Mk 2 aircraft; 849 'B' Flight also returned, but with Gannet AEW Mk 3 aircraft, and 826 NAS with six Wessex Mk 1 replaced 814 NAS. Two Whirlwind Mk 9 helicopters were carried for search and rescue duties, together with a 'COD' Gannet for air freight and passenger duties. Two hundred and twenty officers and some 1,900 men formed the ship's company.

The commission took the ship both east and west of Suez, and included covering the withdrawal from Aden. It has been covered, albeit from a somewhat biased point of view, in a tale entitled 'An Engineer's Bedtime Story', from the ship's Third Commission Book. This is reproduced below to show how one department saw the period. . . .

'Once upon a time there was a big ship with a lop-sided funnel and a flat top, painted a dirty grey with big brown patches, and tied to a wall. She had very few people aboard and even fewer people who knew how the engines worked. One day the Owners decided that this ship must go to sea again (some said for evermore) so they hired the Men of Guzz to work on her.

Much later when the Men of Guzz had left, and later still when the ship looked clean again, she started trials. First she tested her engines to make sure that they would go, and then she tested her seamen to see if they knew which way she ought to go. Finally she tested her engineers to see if they knew why her engines, boilers, generators, catapults and arrester gear went at all. Often doubts remained, but the Owners believed that all would come to pass as it was written in Books of Reference 3000 and 3001; their faith was rewarded, and she went out on to the waters of the world.

Her first voyage took her to Gibraltar, Hamburg and thence almost to Scotland, where chaos fell upon her from the Forth Bridge. All her lights went out, her pumps shook, her gauges quivered, her engines stopped and she was unable to move at all. All her aeroplanes deserted her for their nesting place at Lossie and gloom descended on the M.C.R. (Machinery Control Room).

But her resourceful engineers danced the dance of the water carnival and made burnt offerings to their designers (Newcomen, Watt, Parsons and G. and J. Weir (the only brand)) and a few hours later the ship was able to continue on her way.

After the Reeperbahn and a term at Roedean (Exercise Roedean, 7–14 November 1966 in NW Approaches) she was so much in need of care and protection that the Owners committed her to the dock at Portsmouth. There the Men of Pompey gave the engines the overtime they were paid for, and changed one of the propellers to see if the new one would crack in the same place as the first. Finally she was given clean underwear and sent to try her luck once again in foreign ports.

At length she came again to Gibraltar and was initiated into the Rites of the Water Wash, the Bilge Clean, and the Planned Maintenance. Where-upon her stokers became disenchanted with their designers, (N.W.P. and G. and J.W., (the only brand)) and made obeisance to a new deity called Saint Herbert Lott. He was a very good saint who gave them cans of beer with their fuel and cakes with their aeroplanes and so they took in much fuel and recovered many aeroplanes.

After Gibraltar her Owners decided that the ship should begin her Full Power Trial, and (without stopping, it seemed) she passed rapidly through Malta, Naples and the O.R.I. (Operational Readiness Inspection). Here a Most Important Engineer came on board to inspect her machinery whereupon the air was suddenly no longer conditioned, many of her lights went out and Freon ascended from 6 Juliet A.C.U. (Air Conditioning Unit).

In Malta, the boilers were cleaned again, air conditioning units repaired, and steam was kept up all the time. A fortnight later she went again upon the waters to Athens, called in at Cyprus and then lowered her bowsprings — slipped through the Canal and on and on down the Red Sea to Aden. Here, in a windless wilderness of hot salt water and burning sun she sped hither (launching) and thither (recovering) her aircraft and always searching for a way past the Gates of Gan. Meanwhile she repeated the Rite of the Water Wash and did change the pistons on both her catapults, she renewed many steam joints, changed her main reeves and condenflued her evaporators. Her stokers continued to give thanks to the good Saint Herbert for his beer and his cakes and prayed that he might lead them past the Gates of Gan into the Green Pastures of Singapore where, rumour had it, someone else could clean the . . . boilers!

Finally their prayers were answered and, after 83 days and 83 nights since the Malta S.M.P. (Self Maintenance Period), the ship settled down alongside the wall in S.N.B. (Singapore Naval Base). Here, the stokers drank Tiger Beer and Chinese and Malaysian men demonstrated the Great Singapore Wire Rope Trick on No. 2 main reeve. This was a great mystery, and took a fortnight to unravel.

By now, however, her Owners had realised that the ship had stopped over for three weeks — so they sent her post haste to Hong Kong where jelly-fish choked her strainers and fuel leaked from holes in her tanks. The holes were plugged, the inlets were cleaned and thence she sped to Subic, where a great Lethargy settled slowly over her port catapult. This caused many things to be undone to show they had been done and that there was some health left in her, but the Lethargy stayed until the Goddess of Instrumentation came from Lee and all the Dead Loads were ejected into the sea at Middleslip.

Meanwhile, at Fremantle, the good saint Herbert ran out of cakes and ale, and the ship lifted one leg and paddled back to the inns of Portsmouth. On the way her boilers were cleaned, many steam leaks were repaired, superheater tubes were plugged and much was done so that some of her engineers could wander at leisure over the fair city of Pompey and others go thankfully back to Guzz.

But her Owners did not let her rest for long and

in 30 days she reappeared upon the waters, mending her feed-heaters, cleaning her boilers and repairing all the pumps on which the Men of Pompey had chalked up so much overtime. She rounded the Cape and reached Mombasa, where the Most Important Engineer came on board again. Immediately all the lights went out, the air conditioning failed and nostalgia descended on the M.C.R.

A few days later, a big ship with a lop-sided funnel and a flat top, painted grey with rusty streaks down her sides left Mombasa for a destination unknown and, so the story goes, is still steaming somewhere near the Gates of Gan.'

As a potted version of the period the engineers have covered the ship's movements, and a few of its events. However, one or two of the activities of other departments are possibly worthy of mention! One such story was of the baby found in the 'in tray' of the ship's Air Engineering Officer on Recommissioning Day. He was reported as being somewhat shaken, since he was the ship's senior bachelor! The first fixed wing recovery and launch was made by Commander (Air), in a Tiger Moth. On recovery, the engine refused to stop, and later, propellor swinging was found to be something of a lost art. The first night landing of the commission also found all three oleos of a Sea Vixen wanting! As a work-up for the crash crew the event was perfectly timed, even if the honour of the aircrew was a little dented.

On sailing, the ship also re-started its daily newspaper, the *Hermes Herald*. Throughout the ship's life, contributors from every department with articles, jokes and cartoons, together with extracts from national and international news, played a vital part in keeping up morale and ensuring the ship's company stayed abreast of current events. Captain Lewin also initiated a monthly magazine, entitled *Hermes Families Herald*, for despatch to families whilst the ship was abroad. Supported by succeeding captains of the commission (Captain D G Parker DSO DSC AFC and Captain J D E Fieldhouse GCB GBE ADC), circulation rose to 1,500 copies per month. News of the ship's activities and photographs helped to bring absent menfolk a little nearer to their loved ones while the ship was away.

The Fleet Air Arm contribution to Farnborough 1966 once again came from the air group embarked in *Hermes*. 809 NAS were commanded at the time by Lieutenant Commander Lyn Middleton, later to command HMS *Hermes* during the 1982 Falklands campaign. All embarked squadrons contributed to a spectacular flying demonstration of naval air power. The engineers' tale also omitted (presumably because they were so far below the upper deck?), two of the other events towards the end of 1966. Firstly, there was the persistent Russian minesweeper, which accompanied the ship so continuously that it was allocated duties as planeguard and consort, and secondly, the whale which developed the habit of following the ship at a fixed distance, and spouting during flying stations.

In January 1967, whilst in the Gibraltar area, *Hermes* also participated in the making of a James Bond film, and arrived at Malta to be snubbed by the Maltese government, and the Maltese tugmen. Naval personnel eventually assisted to berth the ship, with a dispute simmering over British government plans for a rundown of British forces in the George Cross island. A visit to Naples in February would be particularly remembered by the ship's outstanding rugby side, who played the local side Portenope. Having agreed to play two halves of 35 minutes at the start of the game, the first half went on for 50 minutes. Half time was spent explaining to the Italian referee just what 35 minutes was in French, German and English, together with a few naval terms. He finally understood and the second half lasted 48 minutes, with a final score of 21—19 to the ship.

February 1967 was also remembered for the 'Case of the Misplaced Flight Deck Officer' (FDO). At flying stations, with one Vixen airborne from each catapult, the FDO noticed a parked and chocked forklift truck obstructing a Vixen taxiing up the flight deck to load for launch. The FDO stopped the Vixen, but with no one apparently coming to move the truck, impatience overcame discretion. He manned the driving seat of the forklift truck, started the motor and attempted to move it. Not having first removed the chocks, his task became a little difficult. Undeterred, FDO gave a touch of forward gear, followed by astern, to jump the chocks holding the forklift. Over the rear chocks he went, and straight over the side, gracefully into space.

The ship turned away, and the rescue helicopter was quickly on the scene. Somewhat bruised, particularly in his pride, the FDO was taken to the sickbay. By the next morning every piece of flight deck machinery had gained an extra marking — 'keep clear of water — no flotation gear fitted'.

After Naples, NATO exercises Poker Hand and Dawn Clear preceded the Malta Self Maintenance Period, followed by a visit to Athens. The Greeks were most courteous, and waited for the ship's departure before having their *coup d'état*. At sea the 1,000th deck landing was achieved during some interesting flying in the Med, particularly with the USS *America*. Cyprus was remembered for the cricket game where the ship's umpire was locked in the lavatory after tea — had it been because he gave the Captain out LBW, or because he had fallen asleep? The Suez Canal was transited, just before it closed, and the ship took up its station off Aden on 6 May 1967, where a complicated and explosive political situation existed. Some exciting flying over the Aden Protectorate followed, where the rugged and arid nature of the terrain was only exceeded by the hostility of the natives. Together with aircraft from *Victorious* and RAF *Khormaksar*, the army and federal government of South Arabia were treated to a demonstration of air power by over 50 aircraft. 826 Squadron aircraft also found themselves operating out of Habilayn, a small airstrip and base 44 miles north-west of Aden, on 'dissident hunting missions'.

On 19 May *Hermes* departed for Singapore, but got no further than Gan before the international situation halted those particular plans. A period of 'wait' and 'continue' led to a fairly famous photograph of *Hermes* prescribing ever-increasing circles on a large portion of the Indian Ocean being linked with a national newspaper reporter's hypothetical signal, reproduced below:

'An abstract from the signal log of HMS *Ubiquitous*, on passage in the Indian Ocean.

C-in-C Singapore to Ubiquitous: Urgent amendment sailing orders. Courtesy call South Africa ports cancelled. Re-embark all coloured personnel and Chinese cooks debarked in anticipation SA visit and alter course for Aden. Render all necessary assistance required by local civil and military authorities to maintain order during disturbances. Report position and estimated time of arrival Aden.

U to C-in-C: Your signal received and understood. Wilco. My position 3.15 N 79.44 E. ETA Aden — early June.

C-in-C to U: Cancel my last signal. Re-debark Chinese cooks and proceed with all possible speed Hong Kong. Make show of strength during civil disturbances. Equip shore patrols with anti-riot weapons. Stand by to take over Hong Kong—Kowloon ferry service from strikers. Report position and ETA Hong Kong.

U to C-in-C: Wilco. Have fetched round to take up easterly course and my position is once again 3.15 N 79.44 E. ETA Hong Kong — Tuesday week.

C-in-C to U: Most urgent. Abandon course Hong Kong and make all possible speed Gulf of Aqaba. Stand by southern approaches to Strait of Tiran outside territorial waters establishing British presence but in view of delicate situation in area establish it with maximum circumspection. Report position and ETA Tiran.

U to C-in-C: Wilco. Have come round on to westerly course again and am back at 3.15 N 79.44 E. ETA Tiran — mid June.

C-in-C to U: Note amendment previous signal. In view local customs and feelings debark Jewish personnel before proceeding Tiran.

U to C-in-C: Wilco. In view possible Papal pronouncement on situation advise whether should keep RCs below decks.

C-in-C to U: Urgent amendment previous signals. Re-embark forthwith all Jewish personnel debark coloured personnel and proceed with maximum despatch Macao. Establish British presence outside territorial waters in support British Council. Report ETA Macao.

U to C-in-C: Wilco. ETA Macao uncertain but expect to be back at 3.15 N 79.44 E in approximately 10 minutes.

C-in-C to U: Urgent re-amendment to amended orders. Political situation United Nations re Aqaba question makes immediate courtesy call African port essential. Debark all white personnel and proceed forthwith Mombasa.

U to C-in-C: Wilco. Advise whether Chinese cooks classified white or coloured in Mombasa.

C-in-C to U: Correction. Proceed Shanghai establish discreet British presence in support two British diplomats being booed by crowd. In view local sensibilities re defectors re-embark Chinese cooks again.

U to C-in-C: Wilco.

C-in-C to U: Cancel last signal. Proceed at once Gibraltar make discreet show of strength outside territorial waters off Algeciras.

U to C-in-C: Show of strength impossible without full complement of Chinese cooks.

C-in-C to U: Re-re-embark Chinese cooks forthwith. Astonished not re-embarked already.

U to C-in-C: Wilco. Advise whether should circumnavigate world eastabout or westabout.

C-in-C to U: Westabout calling at Malta for major refit. Imperative you reassure local population HM Government still using base.

U to C-in-C: Wilco. Have kept helm hard over and am almost back at 3.15 N 79.44 E again.

C-in-C to U: Correction. Proceed eastabout via North-West Passage so as to pass Iceland protect British trawlers suffering harrassment by Icelandic gunboats.

U to C-in-C: Wilco.

C-in-C to U: Your signal very faint.

U to C-in-C: My signalman very dizzy. But British presence at 3.15 N 79.44 E almost overpowering. Situation here entirely under control.

C-in-C to U: Well done *Ubiquitous*. But in view general world feeling de-bark all personnel with British nationality before proceeding further.'

Eventually the ship returned to Aden, and as the Sinai War raged, patrolled off the coast. It was 11 June before the ship was released, and on 22 June gave unrestricted leave for the first time in 66 days. The stay included recording a programme for BBC

Sunday Half Hour Community Hymn Singing and some exciting sport, including athletics. Action followed soon at the next port of call, Hong Kong. During a dawn raid on Communist agitators on 4 August 1967, Wessex helicopters of 826 Squadron lowered police and troops on top of two 27-storey buildings. The ship then moved to Subic, and a story from the army personnel on board for Carrier Borne Ground Liaison. Their account reads:

'Undoubtedly the most memorable day of the third commission for us was the day we went ashore to a place called Wild Horse Creek in the Philippines. The aim was to control the ship's aircraft during five days as they attacked targets on the range nearby. The area was only accessible by helicopter, and the Section, together with the camping equipment, food, water, rations, batteries and other gear required three trips to get it ashore. The first two lifts were uneventful and Private Gilder and the bulk of the stores comprised the last lift. The aircraft was not long airborne when it ditched. Fortunately, there were no casualties as the aircrew and Gilder escaped without difficulty and were winched out of the sea, but the helicopter sank taking with it everything that was vital to the success of the exercise, in the form of both radios, all the food and cooking equipment, and the OC's 'click-click' bed! The exercise was subsequently abandoned and the rest of the Section lifted back to the ship. This was Private Gilder's first trip in a helicopter, and when his feet touched the deck after his rescue he is alleged to have expressed, in true military fashion, to the CO of 826 Squadron that he wished it to be his last!.'

From Subic the ship experienced the fantastic hospitality of the Australians at Fremantle, before an 11,800 mile, fast, non-flying passage round the Cape of Good Hope direct to Portsmouth, arriving on 2 October 1967. Captain Lewin was relieved by Captain D C Parker DSO DSC AFC in October, but not before he had seen the official adoption ceremony of the ship by Tiverton, an association which continued for the rest of the ship's career. After one brief month in the UK the ship turned straight round, and sailed back East of Suez. En route, at Spithead, the ship's company manned the side in strength to cheer ship for the RMS Queen Mary on her last voyage. Ascension and Mombasa were the next ports of call, before a cold Christmas away from home (again) on the Arabian Riviera — Salala, Masirah, Khar el Quwai and Duhar Dibbah. Unfortunately, Captain Parker was taken ill just before arrival in Mombasa, and had to be flown home. He made a full recovery and returned to the ship, again at Mombasa, on 20 January 1968. This unfortunate incident did however enable

Hermes to claim Admiral Sir John Fieldhouse GCB GBE ADC, later to become Chief of Naval Staff and First Sea Lord, as a former commanding officer, he being 'in command' for the month Captain Parker was away.

During this period the closure of the Suez Canal meant a drastic reduction in shipping in the area in which *Hermes* was operating, halfway between the shores of Arabia and Africa. By 1 February 1968 the ship had been allowed to start its homeward journey, and was at Cape Town for a brief visit, returning to Portsmouth on 18 February. Over the next two months, while the ship was prepared for a further period of service at sea, most of the officers and men on board were relieved by those who were to form the ship's company and air groups of the Fourth Commission.

Left Refit 1964 to 1966: Nearly completed and £10 million expended. All guns were removed, and improved catapults were fitted for the Buccaneer and Sea Vixen Mark 2s.

Below, left Captain Lewin joins the padre and some happy dads at a christening on board — using the ship's bell.

Below, right A hangar as no aircraft hangar control officer would wish to see it — nearing the end of the refit.

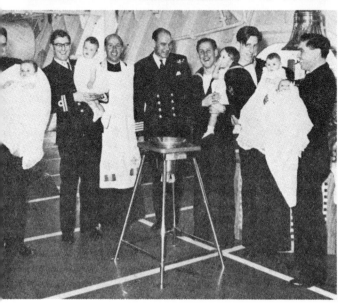

51

16th May 1966 — all systems go, as the orders to make revolutions are passed from the machinery control room . . .

. . . while below, with a tweak of the throttles . . .

*. . . the ship proceeded to sea;
Full Power Trials off the Isle of
Aran, Scotland, summer 1966.*

*The engineering devotees of Saint
Herbert, from the 'Engineers'
Bedtime Story'*

The first launch and recovery of the Third Commission, by Cdr (Air). But was the Tiger Moth really the modern aircraft the ship had been promised?

Perhaps it should be, as a Sea Vixen (**below**) recovering breaks all three oleos.

Facing, above A Buccaneer Mk 2 of 809 Naval Air Squadron, at 50 feet above sea level, at about 600 knots. Note the vapour along the trailing wing edges.

Facing, below A 2-inch rocket attack on a splash target by a Mk 2 Buccaneer

Naval airpower at Farnborough, 1966: 809 NAS in strength

Below *The persistent Russian planeguard 'escorting'* **Hermes** *off Scotland, winter 1966.*

Two flight deck personnel search for the missing flight deck officer and fork lift truck; February 1967.

Below *Operational Readiness Inspection in the Med, March 1967; a Buccaneer poised for launch*

The army and federal government of the Aden Protectorate are treated to a demonstration of air power. The RN air wings of **HMS Victorious** and **Hermes**, together with **RAF Khormaksar** Hunters, overfly **Hermes** and the Aden Protectorate, May 1967.

Below decks, however, while operating off the area, numerous activities were undertaken. Here hopeful contestants await judging of the Cake Making contest.

Fitness was maintained by 'voluntary' massed PT on the flight deck between flying serials.

A floodlit derby, carrier style — on the flight deck, off Aden — maintained morale.

Above, left The ship's own group, 'The Hermites'

Above, right Royal Marine band concert in the hangar

Left Several model-making competitions were held, where standards were high.

Facing, above The picture which is always associated with the 'HMS Ubiquitous/C-in-C' series of signals. **HMS Hermes** prescribes ever-increasing circles in the Indian Ocean, near Gan, May 1967 — during a steering gear breakdown!

Facing, below An artistic picture of **Hermes**, framed against the palm trees of Gan, Indian Ocean, May 1967

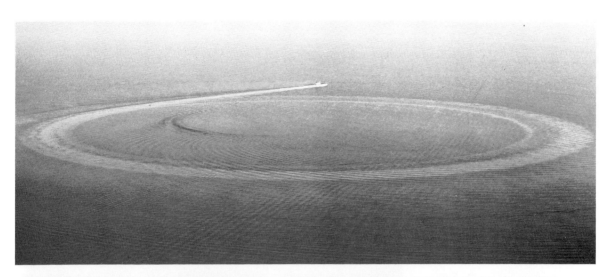

Singapore at last, 22 June to 20 July 1967, and a Veteran's Race, with a famous winner (Captain Lewin) about to collect the prize.

Recording for BBC Sunday half-hour broadcast on the quarterdeck while in Singapore.

Singapore Dockyard's 'Great Singapore Wire Rope Trick' on No 2 arrester wire main reeve; it took two weeks to unravel!

Dawn raid on Communist agitators 4 August 1967 in Hong Kong, by Wessex helicopters of 826 NAS dropping police and troops on top of the suspect buildings, 27 storeys high.

Below *After Hong Kong July/August 1967 the supply officers reassess cash left after over 70 days without unrestricted leave, and with two monumental 'benders' in Singapore and Hong Kong.*

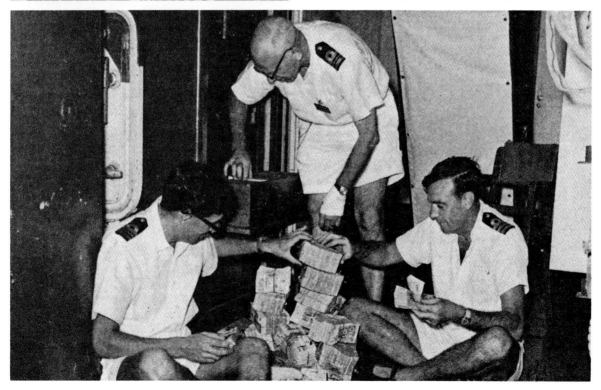

*A six-ship RAS (Replenishment at Sea) off Hong Kong, 7 August 1967. HM ships **Hermes, Minerva** and **Galatea** replenish simultaneously solids and fuel from Royal Fleet auxiliaries **Tideflow, Reliant** and **Retainer**.*

Above Home at last, 2 October 1967; after an
11,500-mile non-stop journey from Fremantle,
Western Australia, **Hermes** returns to Portsmouth.

And after berthing, families flood on board.

One of Captain Lewin's last official acts as Captain, **HMS Hermes**, accepting the official adoption certificate of the ship by Tiverton — an association which continued to the end of the ship's life.

Below Hermes, leaving Spithead, November 1967, passes **RMS Queen Mary** leaving Southampton for the last time, en route to America for conversion to an hotel and conference complex. The ship's company lined the side to give three cheers as she passed.

An end of commission post card — the Photographic Department's artistic interpretation. **Hermes** is off Aden, and the photograph shows squadron crests, with each type of aircraft serving on board in those squadrons embarked during the Third Commission.

Below **Hermes** entering Cape Town, February 1968, after Christmas abroad — in the Gulf. Table mountain is framed in the photograph.

5

Fourth Commission
1968 to 1970

The recommissioning ceremony for the Fourth Commission was held in Portsmouth on 17 May 1968 before many distinguished guests, including Admiral Sir John Bush KCB DSC and Bar, Commander-in-Chief Western Fleet. At the conclusion of the service, and the address by Captain Parker, the cake was cut by the captain's wife, assisted by Mrs Bolt, wife of the ship's master-at-arms.

After storing, the ship proceeded to post-DED trials in the Channel, which included approaches to the ship by one of the Royal Navy's new Phantom aircraft, soon to embark on HMS *Ark Royal*. 'Wings over the Navy' became a well-known photograph of that time — it is in the photographic section at the end of this chapter. Not receiving as much attention were the unarrested landings of the Britten Norman Islander aircraft which, rumour had it, was just about to replace the Captain's Huntress as Captain's Barge!

New squadrons embarked; 814 NAS returned, this time with Wessex Mk 3 anti-submarine helicopters (with the distinctive radar 'hump' behind the engine), 849 'A' Flight replaced 'B' Flight; 801 Squadron Buccaneers replaced 809 NAS, and 893 Squadron Vixens replaced 892 NAS. Work-up was completed in a fog-shrouded Moray Firth, one week's leave was given to each watch, and a swift passage to the Far East followed. The destination was the Penang area, via Gibraltar and Cape Town. The friendly relations of the time with South African defence forces were epitomised by a SAAF Shackleton dropping mail to the ship whilst en route to Cape Town. During the visit *Hermes* was able to farewell the port captain, Captain Aubrey Matson, who for twenty years had guided RN ships in and out of South African ports, and she was the 114th British warship or auxiliary to visit a South African port since the closure of the Suez Canal. Indeed, many thousands of naval personnel, both serving and retired, will recall the enormous hospitality shown over the years to the Royal Navy by the people of South Africa with real affection.

Also on passage, an unusual day's flying was undertaken — a ship's kite-flying competition. Many

unusual contraptions found their way to the flight deck, where most developed a propensity for fan intakes, in preference to the wide open spaces!

Friday 23 August 1968 was an especial VIP visitors' day. First to arrive was Admiral W D O'Brien, ex-captain of *Hermes*, then Commander, Far East Fleet. He was followed closely by Rear Admiral A T F G Griffin CB, Flag Officer Second in Command Far East Fleet. But they were both just in time to welcome the back seat observer of an 803 Squadron Buccaneer from Lossiemouth. This VIO (Very Important Observer), was none other than the First Sea Lord, Admiral Sir Michael Le Fanu KCB CB DSC. The assembly was completed later in the evening with the arrival of Flag Officer Aircraft Carriers, Rear Admiral M F Fell CB DSO DSC and Bar; it must have been somewhat crowded in 4 U Flat that evening!

FOAC had however come to conduct the ship's Operational Readiness Inspection, which, successfully completed, allowed the ship to carry on to a planned visit to Singapore.

FO2FEF embarked for the next phase of the deployment, Exercise Coral Sands: Australia, New Zealand, America and UK all sending ships to participate. Several ships bore more than a passing resemblance to *Hermes*, such as *Albion, Triumph* and HMAS *Sydney*. But after two weeks, where both sides claimed a total annihilation of the other, and with HMNZS *Waikato* nursing a very sore nose after trying to slice through a 30-foot shark, all ships dispersed to various ports in Australia and New Zealand to enjoy a well-earned rest. *Hermes* was fortunate enough to 'draw' Sydney for its port visit and was treated to the fabulous view of the famous harbour, coupled with the legendary hospitality of New South Wales. Almost all messes on board became festooned with 'rabbits', from koalas to boomerangs, and the ship's company were hard-pressed to take up all the offers of entertainment by the friendly 'natives'.

Jervis Bay, south of Sydney and near the Australian Naval Air Base Nowra (HMAS *Albatross*) was the next operating area, with *Hermes* being visited by

RAN S2 Trackers and A4 Skyhawks. The ship left one mark on Nowra: a Gannet one night tried quite successfully to eat its way through a hangar, after brake failure while taxiing. A sick-looking culprit was retrieved later, by lighter from Sydney, but the Vixen which diverted on the last day with airframe problems did not rejoin until later, after a long sea voyage to Singapore!

Okinawa, with its US naval airbase of Naha, was the next port of call, before the last visit to Hong Kong by a fixed wing carrier of the RN Far East Fleet. What could be called the first road runners were christened 'the *Hermes* Harriers' and took part in various attempts to capture the title of 'fastest Hong Kong Hilton Hotel to Peak' road racers. Eventually their efforts were crowned with success, which is more than can be said for the efforts of various pilots, who were given a 'crash' course in driving army vehicles in the New Territories. Their only recorded success was in their attempt to think in two dimensions, instead of the normal three!

Christmas 1968 was spent in Singapore, where Operation 'Mistletoe' was crowned with success, despite the crash of the charter firm British Eagle, who were supposed to bring the wives and sweethearts of the ship's company out for Christmas. Credit where due, the RAF turned up trumps and flew the girls out somehow on their scheduled flights; 'Santa Claus' indeed.

After Christmas, the exercise Fotex saw the ship's 2,000th deck landing of the commission, witnessed by the Commander Far East Fleet, who was at sea with the ship for the day. The exercise was in fact noteworthy for the amount of cross-operating which took place. *Hermes* Buccaneers were striking Fleet units defended by RAF and RAAF fighters; Vixens used RAF tanker aircraft before being taken under control of RAAF ground controllers; they then intercepted RAAF Mirages striking under RN Gannet control. Fotex also saw operations by 32 ships from four navies (RN, RAN, RNZN, and RMN). This was war of the gentler sort however, as the programme was planned with time for weekend banyans with fishing competitions off Penang. Title of Ship's Paramount Piscatorial Predator went to the angler on board who landed a 4-oz monster of smoked haddock genus, but doubtful origin.

After Fotex there was time only for a very brief stop at Singapore, as the last Fixed Wing Carrier Visit of the Far East Fleet to HM naval base Singapore, before a fast passage back to Australia, this time to Fremantle in Western Australia. Time was taken on passage to hold an extraordinary horse racing meeting on the flight deck on Saint Valentine's Day, where the betting was brisk, even if the horses weren't. Cyclone 'Gladys', which paid close attention to the ship during this passage, put paid to most of the planned flying programme.

Fremantle and Perth proved as hospitable as ever, with over one thousand sailors, with a similar number of guests, attending a ship's company dance during the visit — quite some party one imagines! Cape Town was visited on the way home, for another good run, on a cruise which had been noted by those on board for its good runs, and the ship sailed with a farewell from the mayor of Cape Town which said 'Come back any time, you will be welcome'.

On the passage home the ship was told of the promotion to Flag Rank of Captain Parker, and arrived home in high spirits to a welcome from literally thousands of families on a bitterly cold 1 April 1969. *Hermes* had been away nearly nine months and had steamed 59,000 miles; she now came home to rest briefly in 'D' lock during DED until September 1969, with her ship's company accommodated on board HMS *Centaur*.

Captain (later Rear Admiral) P M Austin assumed command on 2 July 1969, while the ship, among many other activities, was repainted completely, both inside and out. All on board looked as new for the rededication service on 29 August, which was combined with Families Day, before sailing on 2 September 1969. Squadrons re-embarked after sea trials, 814 Squadron first, before the new flight deck paint started getting scuff marks from wire arrests again. An intensive period of flying off Scotland followed, as new aircrew and ship's company relearned how to operate the smallest deck in the world 'to launch and recover' such sophisticated aircraft, of such size and speed as the 801 Mk 2 Buccaneers and 893 Mk 2 Vixens. During this time however a weekend was spent at Rosyth. Tides were not that favourable — anchoring to await low tide to pass under the Forth Bridge on the way up was followed by anchoring again to wait for high tide to go alongside. At least it was a chance for the 'Northern Natives' to get home — and the rest of the ship's company to savour the delights of Edinburgh.

Hughie Green's 'Opportunity Knocks' was broadcast live from the hangar during an AMP in Portsmouth in November 1969, before Exercise Decamp in the eastern Atlantic with HMS *Eagle*. The scenario for this exercise was the struggle between the opposing fatherlands of Austinland (*Hermes*: Captain Austin) and Treacherterra (*Eagle*: Captain Treacher). That Austinland was going to war was, of course, due to the unprovoked naked agression by the naval jackals of Treacherterra. It became essential to deliver a punitive lesson of air superiority through the medium of the steely-eyed lantern-jawed patriots on board. Confident apparently that an Austinland victory would prevail, the supposed neutral observer forces of Focasia embarked in *Hermes* to observe the fray. Initially the scene was set by a pre-dawn strike by an 801 Buccaneer. Rapidly finding its target, it then landed on, where its 'delayed-action peace gas bombs' destroyed the enemy's will to resist. Soon the *Eagle* had become fully Austinised, when Focasia asked for help from both carriers to 'destroy' five RFAs, all of whom were making their way to Gibraltar by devious routes south of the two carriers. Four RFAs were soon discovered, but *Lyness* was a gallant enemy, and remained unseen until succumbing in time to permit entry into Gib for the weekend! Surrounded by captured RFAs, and a subdued *Eagle, Hermes* entered Gibraltar on 28 November 1969.

Christmas 1969 was, for a change, spent at Portsmouth, before the final deployment of the commission, into the Mediterranean from January to June 1970. An unenviable 'first' for the Fleet Air Arm followed at sea, however, when the ship was the first to exercise the new Martin Baker rocket-powered ejection seat from the flight deck! The cause was a Buccaneer on the port catapult, which, just before launch, and with full power applied, broke loose from its hold back and accelerated to launch without the benefit of catapult assistance. On reaching the bow, the Buccaneer dropped straight into the sea, becoming a focus of attention for a watching Soviet spy trawler. Pilot and observer were safely recovered, however, thanks to the new ejection seat.

During this deployment the ship carried out two planned maintenance periods in Grand Harbour Malta, with squadrons disembarked to RAF bases ashore, at this time RAF Luqa. Rumour most unkindly has it that the RAF pilots and navigators attached to *Hermes* Air Group were not sure whether to be flattered or embarrassed at being classed as naval officers in an RAF mess, and settled for schizophrenia! Visits were paid to Villefranche, for all to lose their shirts at the nearby casinos of Monaco, and to Istanbul, where the ship embarked vast quantities of cossack hats and suede and leather coats. Off Malta, on the return passage, the MV *Earner*, an ex-RN minesweeper, was given assistance after breakdown in heavy weather. Without this help, it would most likely have foundered.

Hermes returned to the UK on 22 June 1970, via a Families Day, to enter refit and end her fixed wing role, as part of government policy at the time to run down the Fleet Air Arm. 893 Squadron, formed with Fulmars and Martlets in 1942, and much in evidence since with first Sea Venoms and then Sea Vixens, was to disband. Also to go was *Hermes'* first squadron, 814 NAS. In the Fourth Commission, the ship had spent over 8,000 hours underway in a little over two years; she had steamed nearly 126,000 miles. She was however to be placed into preservation, her ship's company progressively reduced, and finally suffered the indignity of being towed to Devonport for conversion to a helicopter carrier, a task which was to last until August 1973.

Facing A famous photograph of the time: one of the Royal Navy's new Phantom aircraft, soon to be embarked in **HMS Ark Royal**, overflies **Hermes** during post DED (Docking Essential Defect) trials in the Channel, May/June 1968.

Top Captain D G Parker DSO DSC AFC, reading the Commissioning Warrant, 17 May 1968.

Above The Commissioning Cake produced for the occasion

Above 'Hands to Bathe' during a quiet period,
19 June 1968, en route for the Far East . . . Did
someone say 'shark'?

Left Crossing the Line again, 26 June 1968, en route
for Cape Town

Facing, above Entering Cape Town, the 114th
British warship/auxiliary to enter since the closure
of the Suez Canal.

Facing, below Oops, a nose wheel collapse on landing
by an 893 Squadron Vixen; pilot Lieut Price RN,
Observer F O McNeil Matthews RAF; 12 August
1968.

Above An 814 NAS Wessex overflies Sydney
Harbour Bridge, 14 October 1968.

Below Departing Fremantle, Western Australia,
homeward bound, 27 February 1969.

Facing, above The last Far East Fleet fixed wing
carrier enters Singapore Naval Base, 30 August 1968.

Facing, below The COD Gannet lands on — with
mail — during Exercise Coral Sea, en route for
Sydney, Australia; 2-14 October 1968.

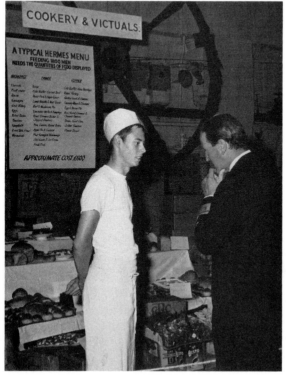

Above *A combined Rededication- and Families Day was held on 29 August 1969, after the DED, under new management. Captain P M Austin having assumed command on 2 July 1969.*

Left *Rear Admiral M F Fell CB DSO DSC and Bar, Flag Officer Carriers and Amphibious Ships, discusses catering at a Families Day cookery stand with Cook Hayes from the main galley; 29 August 1969.*

Facing *Back at sea, 849 Squadron Airborne Early Warning Gannets (above) re-embark in Lyme Bay, 25 September 1969 . . .*

. . . and join in time for some heavy weather (below). Rough seas in the Moray Firth, viewed from the quarterdeck on 29 September 1969.

Facing, above 'Opportunity Knocks' showgirls get down to scrubbing the flight deck; a programme was televised on board at Portsmouth on 9 November 1969.

Facing, below Exercise Decamp, November 1969; a weary Buccaneer observer leaves his 801 Squadron aircraft after a night **Austinland** strike on Treacher-terra (alias **HMS Eagle**).

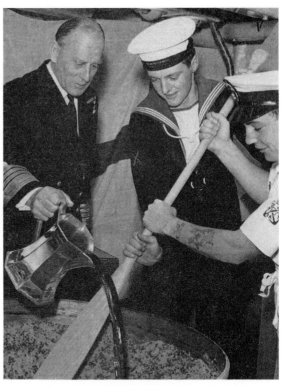

Right While in Gibraltar, Admiral Sir John Bush, Governor and CINC Gibraltar, visits the ship and adds a certain flavour to the Christmas pudding mix; 3 October 1969. Cook Drummond and Junior Seaman Nesbitt assist . . .

. . . while below, the main cafeteria cook duty watch 'await the locusts'.

Above Returning to the Med in February 1970, after Christmas leave. **Hermes** flies Admiral Bush's flag, Union Flag at the jackstaff, and harbour ensign, as she carries out a ceremonial steam past Gibraltar on the admiral's departure as Governor and Commander-in-Chief.

Seacat missile firing, 15 March 1970

Close to the casinos at Ville-franche, 24 March 1970 . . .

. . . a children's party is also held . . .

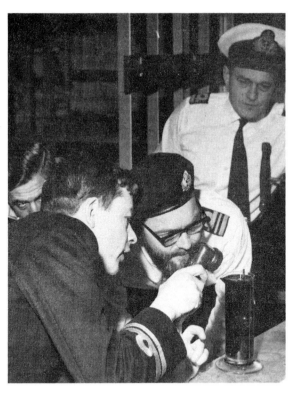

Left A matter of the utmost importance, as supply officers of the Fourth Commission conduct a density test on the rum stock in the Spirit Room; 13 April 1970.

Below Entering Grand Harbour Malta; 14 April 1970

Facing, above left Istanbul, 14 May 1970: a dancer entertains some of the Ship's Company ashore.

Facing, above right The **MV Earner** incident off Malta; a helicopter lowers salvage teams and equipment; June 1970.

Facing, below A June 1970 Mediterranean replenishment by both RN and USN.

Left Vixens of 893 Squadron, who left **Hermes** on 21 June 1970 to disband, overfly the ship in the 'Big H' formation for the last time . . .

Right . . . before making their way in pairs to their base at NAS Yeovilton.

Below Despite the fact that she was about to be towed to Devonport for conversion, as can be seen from this 1970 Navy Days picture, she was the public's favourite.

6

Conversion to a commando role
1970 to 1976

Although she returned to Portsmouth in June 1970, it was not until March 1971 that work began on the conversion which was to fit *Hermes* as a successor to HMS *Albion*, in the commando role, whilst retaining the secondary role of anti-submarine helicopter carrier.

The job was one of the biggest that Devonport dockyard had undertaken in years, costing between £12 and £15 million at 1970 prices. It involved stripping the flight deck to remove the arrester wires used by jet aircraft and the two steam catapults used to launch them. Elsewhere, the giant radar scanner on top of the bridge was removed and replaced by a single 'bedstead' radar aerial; below decks, major changes were made to the hangar to fit it to take vehicles for the Royal Marine Commando which, with its supporting Royal Artillery Battery, could number over 900 men. The hangar was also to be used by the Wessex 5 Commando helicopters, up to 16 of them. The galley, laundry, and bakery were all modernised, as was the air conditioning, and major alterations made to the accommodation to enable *Hermes* to take the commandos on board. Extra space also had to be found for their weapons and kit. Four new landing craft were to be carried, outboard below flight deck level, and this involved cutting out a small segment of the angled deck to take the davits. The flight deck was strengthened to take the new Harrier GR1 aircraft, forerunner of the Sea Harrier, while the Operations Room was completely updated. All this work was to have been completed in two years, though, in the event, a Royal Dockyard strike did cause a short extension to this plan.

Captain C R P C Branson assumed command on 26 February 1973 and post-refit sea trials were undertaken most successfully in May 1973. During this period, a 250-gallon Avcat spillage in the hangar necessitated 'emergency stations' for real, during which the ship's company played the dockyard team, 650 strong, at deck hockey! The resulting score is not recorded, neither is a photograph held of what must have been an incredible sight.

Prior to recommissioning, the existing links with Tiverton were further strengthened when the Borough Council decided unanimously on 13 November 1972 to confer on the Captain, officers and ship's company of HMS *Hermes* the Honorary Freedom of the Borough. The official resolution says that this was 'in recognition of the glorious achievements of the Royal Navy, both in peace and war, and in appreciation of the close and cordial association between HMS *Hermes* and the town of Tiverton which had existed in recent years'. These links had, of course, begun in a modest way when Tiverton Sea Cadet Unit, formed in 1943, was renamed TS *Hermes* in 1959. Exchanges of visits by cadets, mayors, councillors and members of the ship's company had continued the connection, and the ship had been formally adopted by the town in 1968.

The Freedom Ceremony, with formal presentation of the scroll and an engraved casket, took place in Tiverton on 19 July 1973. There to witness the event were two former commanding officers of the ship, Vice Admiral T T Lewin and Rear Admiral D G Parker. Also present was Major General J I H Owen OBE, Major General Royal Marine Commando Forces, marking the ship's new role, as were the Wessex 5 helicopters from 707 Squadron who overflew the event. Two guards from the ship, one naval ratings and the other Royal Marines, and platoons from all sections of the ship then marched past the Captain and the Mayor with bayonets fixed and colours flying.

Two thousand people crowded into the hangar on 18 April 1973 when the ship recommissioned at Devonport. Four previous captains attended: Vice Admiral Lewin, then Vice Chief of Naval Staff; Rear Admiral P M Austin, then Flag Officer Naval Air Command; Captain D S Tibbets, the first Captain; and Admiral Sir William O'Brien. Lady Mary Soames, daughter of Lady Churchill, who had launched *Hermes* at Barrow in 1953, was the guest of honour, and the service was held exactly 60 years after the first flight of an aircraft with folding wings from a vessel at sea. That vessel was, of course, the 8th HMS *Hermes*.

During this period also, some 700 Plymouth schoolchildren swarmed on board for a sponsored flight deck walk. Over £2,500 was raised as innumerable laps were completed.

Having been refitted as a commando carrier, the first major exercise carried out was, needless to say, an ASW one, Exercise Swiftmove. Old friends, in the shape of 814 Squadron, now reformed with Sea Kings, accompanied by 819 and 824 NAS, came on board, as did a detachment of 845 Squadron's Wessex 5s for familiarisation. Over 900 hours were flown during the exercise in October, accompanied by much Russian interest. Some excitement was generated when a shadowing Russian Kanin class destroyer had an explosion and fire on board, and launched a torpedo, presumably to remove it from the scene of the fire. Luckily, the torpedo missed everybody, and the ship's offer of assistance was declined!

After Swiftmove, *Hermes* visited Oslo and was honoured by a visit from King Olav of Norway, formally dressed in uniform — in his rank of Admiral Royal Navy (Honorary). A role change to Commando Carrier (LPH) followed in Devonport in November. Work-up was carried out with 800 pairs of boots occupied by men of 45 Commando off Arbroath, Wester Ross, and then Skye. About 90 of the ship's company will always remember this work-up, when they were taught the joys, and terrors, of abseiling in the Cuillins by 'Royal', courtesy of 845 taxi service.

Christmas 1973 was spent at Devonport, but sailing was delayed a day, due to strong winds. This led to the now unusual sight of two carriers leaving Devonport on one tide, as the ship went out with HMS *Bulwark*. 45 Commando embarked at Rosyth, but only after a harrowing night during which the ship dragged her anchors in gale force winds in the Forth and snagged them in fathoms of old wire. The following narrative entered the Wardroom line book of the time:

'Bridge, Foscle;'
'Bridge;'
'This is Foscle; the First Lieutenant says there will be a slight delay in anchoring;'
'How long?'
'Wait one;'
'Bridge, Foscle;'
'Bridge;'
'About five or six hours; the First Lieutenant says to tell the Captain that there's a bit of wire or something wrapped around the anchor;'
'Well drop the other one;'
'Can't, 'cos it's tied to the first one;'

When the wire problem was sorted out all was not over, since the height of the tide meant that *Hermes* could not escape to the open sea past the Forth Bridge, and an anxious night was spent with the ship

manoeuvering in the confined space, unable to anchor.

Safely away via Narvik, to land the commando, another exciting night was experienced in restricted fjord waters, before Portsmouth was reached for an AMP. En route to recover the Marines, the ship was diverted to participate in the search for the missing trawler *Gaul*. *Hermes* went to the Bear Island area, alas without success. The weather was quite appalling and necessitated a weekend stood down, to repair storm damage, before resuming the LPH role and a frenetic pattern of flying, assaults and withdrawals in fjords infested with submarines and fast patrol boats. Much experience of the fury of an Atlantic snowstorm and arctic 'whiteout' was gained, and the value of arctic survival training brought home to all who ventured ashore.

Warmer climes were ahead however, and, via the delights of Hamburg and the Reeperbahn, *Hermes* entered the Mediterranean and spent April at Malta, reunited with many wives and girlfriends who had flown out. Except for those caught up in Admiral A D Cassidi's harbour inspection, a relaxing three week period was had, before sailing for Cyprus and Greek waters to carry out Exercise Dawn Patrol — a NATO exercise involving five different navies and many ground forces. Apparently the Italian ASW helicopter crew radio transmissions with a mixture of English, Italian and Verdi had to be heard to be believed, but were much enjoyed.

41 Commando embarked for a trip across 'the pond' (the Atlantic), to New Brunswick, Canada, and disappeared into the backwoods for Exercise Black Swan, accompanied by 845 Squadron. This was enlivened from time to time by seven-foot-tall Canadian black bears, who tried to sleep in the bivouacs and stay to supper! *Hermes* however sat in Halifax and tried to maintain herself, before going to the Bermuda area for the Canadian exercise Marcot, with Canadian HS 50 (Sea King) aircraft embarked to join 814 Squadron. 41 were then recovered and taken to share in the delights of a New York visit over Fourth of July celebrations. Lynn Redgrave and Jim Dale were among many, many visitors to the ship in a really good visit.

The plan was then to return 41 Commando to its home base in Malta and go home, but plans went somewhat awry with the Turkish invasion of Cyprus. 41 were eventually landed to support British Sovereign Base Areas in Cyprus, while *Hermes* steamed into the Turkish war danger zone off Kyrenia to evacuate British and other refugees in northern Cyprus on 23 July 1974. Altogether, British military forces rescued 7,526 people, 5,171 of them British. 845 Squadron's helicopters, assisted by others, such as *Devonshire*'s Wessex 3, ran a shuttle taxi service to the ship, where sailors were ready with everything from hot showers to babies' creches, hot tea to warm clothing. Ashore,

British army armoured cars escorted convoys of cars laden with refugees to the embarkation area. One Greek Cypriot woman, who had given birth and was evacuated with her two-day-old baby girl, was so moved that she christened her daughter Hermoula, the feminine form of Hermes.

After the evacuation *Hermes* moved to lie off the Sovereign Base Area at Akrotiri, where the refugees were off-loaded, and 41 re-embarked to return to Malta. A well-earned DAMP at Devonport was then carried out from August to September.

The Dutch were the ship's next international visitors, when the 'Cloggies', alias No 1 ACG of the Royal Netherlands Marine Commandos, came on board for Exercise Northern Merger, an amphibious exercise on NATO's northern flank, assaulting Jutland. Time was found on completion for a visit to wonderful, wonderful Copenhagen, and the Little Mermaid (expensive but enjoyable), before some funny rigs were seen decontaminating in Exercise County Fair. The 'long route' was taken home to allow time to sample the delights of the French way of life in Cherbourg. *Hermes* then returned to Portsmouth, where Captain (later Rear Admiral) Branson was relieved by Captain D R Reffell.

A swift introduction to the ship was afforded the new Captain, as the ship's role changed to ASW for a Joint Maritime Course round the North Atlantic race track. Six Sea Kings of 824 Squadron embarked, with two from 819, and most of 845 Squadron had to get off to make room. The First Sea Lord embarked briefly to view the success of the role change, but the next VIP was seen on the passage to Plymouth. This was Lieutenant The Prince of Wales, in a Wessex 5 of The Red Dragon Flight, for DLPs (Deck Landing Practices), at the culmination of his Commando Operational Flying Training. He was to join 845 Squadron, and embark in *Hermes* on the next deployment. December 74 to end February 75 were taken off for DED in Devonport, a major turn-round in personnel, both senior and junior, and some much-needed maintenance.

42 Commando were the next visitors, for a Westlant deployment, and 845 returned with their newest officer and his Red Dragon Flight. The story has been told by Prince Charles against himself that, at this time, there was great competition among the Marines to travel in his helicopter. When the late Lord Mountbatten heard about this, he remarked 'I can't understand why they should want to fly with one of the least experienced of the pilots. They would do much better going with one of the more senior pilots'.

One detachment of 845 had, however, somehow got themselves away to Puerto Rico and did not rejoin until the ship reached the other side of 'the pond'. They said they were glad to be back, but of course they were not believed, since they had gone completely 'native'.

The American 38th Marine Amphibious Unit was embarked for Exercise Rum Punch on 29 March 1975, and pilots had the opportunity for cross-operating on four makes of US helicopters, including the AH1J Huey Cobra, which was much enjoyed. Almost before *Hermes* had finished waving American friends good-bye, Dutch ones returned for Exercise Van Gogh, preceded by a visit to Curacao and followed by one to Aruba, both of too short a duration. Fort Lauderdale (Florida) followed, for visits to Disneyworld and Miami. All savings of Local Overseas Allowance were dissipated and general hospitality enjoyed, the pattern being set with a nine helo flypast on arrival, flying the Union Jack, Stars and Stripes, the White Ensign and 42 Commando flag.

The ship trecked north from Florida, up to Canada. Once there, 845 deployed ashore to the Gagetown, New Brunswick, training area, while 42 Commando headed for the Blue Mountain and Hibernia training grounds. *Hermes* stayed at Navy Yard Halifax, Nova Scotia, for maintenance, before recovering all absentees and rounding off Westlant 75 with visits to Montreal and Quebec. The berth in Montreal provided excellent views of the Expo '67 site, much of which was still in use as conference facilities, and the site of the 76 Olympics could be seen taking shape. Although a fair hike, many made the effort to take coach tours to the Niagara Falls before, under clear blue skies, the ship headed for Quebec with a VIP team aboard — headed by the British High Commissioner for Canada, Sir John Johnstone. A Farnborough-type Air Day was conducted, *Hermes*-style, for the VIPs and most of the residents of the banks of the St Lawrence River, before berthing at Wolfe's Cove below the Heights of Abraham for a most enjoyable visit — and the incident of being impounded.

Early on the evening of the last day of the visit to Quebec, as the result of an incident ashore, a civilian lawyer actually served a writ on the ship, impounding it until his case was heard. Two junior ratings, one sailor and one Marine, had been involved in a fracas ashore. A civilian had been injured, the ratings were accused, and the lawyer did not believe they would be able to afford his claim for damages. He served the writ on the ship as a safer bet.

As can be imagined, the airwaves between Quebec and London burned hot that night — in the event the ship sailed on schedule, but left two ratings behind. They were, on appearing in court, totally acquitted of all charges, but it made for a most interesting and instructive last evening in port for some. The actual writ is now believed to be in the possession of Vice Admiral Sir Derek Reffell, but when cancelling the writ against *Hermes* it is understood that the judge awarded costs against the civilian lawyer who had started it all, saying 'and when I say costs against you,

I do not mean against your client, I mean you, personally, for having tried to misuse the law'.

On leaving Quebec and sailing down the St Lawrence Seaway, the commando's drivers embarked upon the usual evolution of re-arranging and securing the trailers for the Atlantic crossing. In the course of this operation one trailer, containing a rifle company's set of radio equipment, complete, and very expensive, was moved to the centre of the flight deck — except that the driver neglected to apply the handbrake. A small alteration in course, and the trailer started to roll. Now, it so happened that there was a guard rail around the whole of the flight deck, except of course for one small gap, just about the size of a trailer, just by the forward lift. All stood transfixed as the trailer rolled sweetly through the gap, and over the side.

Later in the crossing the ship had the usual 'Sod's Opera', in which a seaman recounted a conversation between two fishes in the St Lawrence Seaway:

First Fish: 'Have you seen the film about HMS *Hermes* yet?'
Second Fish: 'No, but I have seen the trailer, and if that is anything to go by, it should be a jolly good film!'

Before the ship had sailed for the deployment, it had been agreed to try to raise £650 for the Plymouth group, the Riding for the Disabled Association, a task entitled 'Project 650'. Raffles and sponsored walks were undertaken, culminating in the village fete held on the flight deck on 21 June, but especially focusing on the evening SRE programme. This quickly caught the imagination, when a record was played continuously, until a cash bid from a mess replaced it with their choice. A musical battle developed between the squadrons, the embarked force and the senior ratings messes. The 'Dambusters' theme proved exceedingly popular, and despite efforts to buy it off the air, it always seemed to return. All this hard work and generosity resulted in not £650, but £1,562 being presented on the ship's return.

The citizens of Plymouth were awakened in the early morning of 26 June 1975 by the sound of 845 Wessex 5 helos disembarking 42 Commando to Bickleigh. Sadly, though, when the 845 left, so too did HRH The Prince of Wales, ending six months of being a full member of the squadron. All wished he had been able to stay longer — the ship still treasures the two beautiful cut crystal decanters he presented, engraved with the words 'Red Dragon at Sea — February to June 1975', the ship's crest and the Prince of Wales' crest. Summer maintenance at Devonport followed, before 40,000 people poured on board the ship for Navy Days 1975 at Devonport.

On 1 September *Hermes* sailed for Malta, sunny climes, and a rendezvous with 41 Commando. The ship was joined en route by a green parrot, who seemed oblivious to funnel eruptions or low flying Nimrod aircraft. There were those suspicious individuals on board who suspected a staff spy, but no positive confirmation was received. With 41 safely on board, a pre-exercise conference was held at Istanbul for 'Deep Express', noted not only for the variety and number of officers of different nationalities and services who embarked, but for the number of ship's company who passed them en route heading off the ship for the beaches. After a 'turnaway' landing rehearsal at Doganby Bay, the main assault was reached and only exceeded in scale by the assault on the covered bazaar at Istanbul after the exercise.

Much planning also went into the next serial, that of getting wives and girlfriends out to the AMP in Malta in October, where the visit was marked and marred by the crash of an RAF Vulcan bomber. Witnessed by many from the ship, the aircraft overshot from RAF Luqa, burning fiercely from its starboard side, before exploding in mid-air. The main part of the wreckage landed in a field near the village of Zabbar, though one wing came down in the village street. Fortunately, civilian casualties were few, and the two pilots had been able to eject. They were picked up from the sea by an 814 Squadron helicopter, and ten minutes later were at Mtarfa Military Hospital. The ship also assisted by providing medical and salvage teams.

A brief stop at Guzz followed, just to tantalise natives on board, especially when the ship moved to 'C' Buoy, before participation in Exercises Moby Dick and Ocean Safari. Almost all the Wessex 5s had to be landed, as *Hermes* 'went ASW' and embarked Sea Kings of 819, 826 and 737 Squadrons, to join her own 814 helos. The exercises involved working in the Iceland—Faroes Gap, where some spectacularly rough seas were found, and old lessons relearned about the ability of the helicopter to waltz on the flight deck in such conditions. Rosyth for wash-up and de-brief was greeted with relief by many at the end of November, before maintenance, leave and Christmas at Devonport to round off 1975.

The final deployment before refit was back to the northern flank of NATO, in support of 42 Commando. They joined the ship by air from Arbroath, together with some very 'new look' Sea Kings of 814 Squadron, extensively modified for cold weather operations. Instead of avoiding snow showers, or being grounded, they now went looking for bad weather, which of course was readily available. Temperatures rapidly dropped as the ship moved north, and steam heating and cold weather clothing were welcome in the firmly below zero temperatures. The next two months were largely spent in the area, including some spectacular scenery (and some more grey hairs for the navigator) among the fjords. Time did, however, permit a quick dash away to Cherbourg and Portsmouth, but en route back, the ship's consort (RFA *Regent*) was delayed sailing with engine problems. A diversion to the Plymouth areas followed for a most unusual RAS (Solids) by Vertrep, with *Hermes* at sea, and the RFA alongside. Experienced carrier men will find it no surprise that, despite the delay of the diversion, the navigator found enough time in hand to make the original planned ETA in Norway. Exercise Atlas Express paired 42 Commando, supported by the ship and 845, with Brigade North as Orange, and ranged against them was the Allied Mobile Force of ACE (Allied Command Europe). After this last major exercise concluded, 42 Commando were recovered from Narvik on 17 March and taken to Rosyth, before *Hermes* paid a last foreign visit to Copenhagen. A 'Shop Window' for 350 VIPs on each of two days was undertaken on 6 and 7 April 1976, off Portsmouth, where the ship assisted in demonstrating some of the maritime, air and amphibious capabilities available to NATO. HMS *Lowestoft*, RFA

Olna, HMS *Sabre* and the Dutch conventional submarine *Zwaardvis* also participated, as did RAF Nimrod, Buccaneer, Phantom, Harrier and Canberra aircraft. It all made for two very busy but quite spectacular days, which went off very well, before some 70 sons of the ship's company joined for the trip down to Plymouth.

The final day at sea was spent with families on board, where a polished flying display, fine weather and the RM band all helped to make it an ideal finale to the commission. Devonport for refit was to be the venue for the remainder of the year, to re-emerge as a CVS anti-submarine carrier, and the ship said farewell to its Captain on 27 May 1976, leaving Commander (later Captain) Peter Erskine, the Executive Officer, in command.

Conversion to the Commando Carrier rôle at Devonport, 1971-73

Early 1973: the hangar control officer surveys the state of his empire during the refit.

before . . .

after . . .

'Full house' for the re-commissioning ceremony

Tiverton, 19 July 1973, the occasion of the granting of the Freedom of the Borough. The Freedom Scroll is read to the assembly in the presence of the commanding officer, Captain C R K Branson.

With bayonets fixed and flags flying, the ship 'exercises its rights' in Tiverton on 19 July 1973.

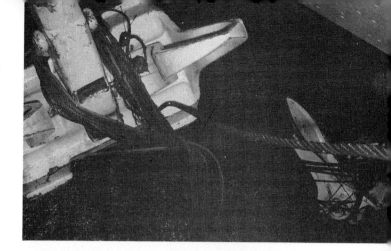

Facing, above The shadowing Russian Kanin destroyer — which discharged a torpedo after an explosion and fire on board — shadows **Hermes** during Exercise Swift Move, October 1973.

Facing, below King Olav of Norway, being greeted by Captain Branson, during his visit on board in Oslo, October 1973.

Right The 'Rosyth Ropewire Trick', 15 January 1974 . . . which caused an 'interesting conversation' and evolution in consequence.

Below Hermes participating in Exercise Clockwork off Norway, March 1974.

Fun in the sun snow . . .

We watch them . . .

watching us . . .

watching them . . .
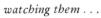

Facing, above *Malta was somewhat warmer . . .*

Facing, below *Some well-known faces came to visit . . .*

96

Facing, above The Turkish invasion of Cyprus, and the evacuation of British and other refugees by *Hermes* on 23 July 1974. A British Army armoured car escorts a refugee convoy to a helicopter pick-up point and the safety of the ship (*below*) off the coast.

Right The 'Cloggies' — enough to turn an RSM grey . . .

Below Painted and prepared, the Dutch helo 'Sticks' take passage to the flight deck for an assault ashore.

Pastimes at sea . . .

Above *The flight deck fête (**left**) — £1,500 was raised! . . . and (**right**) a decontamination exercise — just in case.*

Right *Others took up musical pursuits. Sergeant Otlers Missons, with his famed 'flat-cornered urinicorn'.*

Right 'Welcome on board'. Captain Reffell meets a new, and very different, junior officer.

Below Technical discussions? Lieutenant The Prince of Wales having obviously detailed discussions on basic flight principles with his crew members.

Above To the USA . . . where 'someone' seemed to do well.

Right and below Roughers!

Facing The ship's most famous pilot also tried his hand as chief parking attendant — The Flight Deck Officer.

102

His 500th Flying Hour was celebrated in true naval fashion . . .

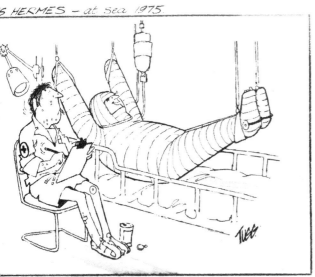

.. DEAR MUM — GUESS WHO LANDED ON ME THIS MORNING ??!!.....

... 'E'S GOT A TERRIFIC SENSE OF 'UMOUR THEY SAID — LET YOUR IMAGINATION RUN RIOT!.....

... *and cartoonists had a field day.*

... YOU'LL NEVER GET A GAME OF POLO NOW! .....

Back in northern waters . . . 'Imagine you're in Singapore' — the chief said . . .

Left Something different — Full Astern trials

Right That famous lady — the Little Mermaid of Copenhagen — sporting a new line in headgear.

7

Return to the CVS role
1976 to 1980

Hermes spent May to December 1976 undergoing a short refit at Devonport, to re-emerge as a CVS, or anti-submarine support ship, her new Commanding Officer, Captain (later Vice Admiral) R C A Fitch, joining on 21 September. He was swiftly to become acquainted with the ship's Tiverton links, as *Hermes* had already organised a Freedom Parade in its affiliated town nine days later. The refit was undertaken during one of the hottest summers on record, and many expeds and charity walks from the Pennine trail to Dartmoor were undertaken in fine weather.

Completion day was 10 December, with Admiral Sir Edward Ashmore, First Sea Lord, honouring the ship with a visit. Post-refit sea trials followed, a bit of a shock for some on board, after several months at home! More sea trials followed in January, before Harrier trials off Plymouth, the Moray Firth and the north-east coast of England. This period offered a preview of the way things would be when the Sea Harrier entered service.

'Portland for work-up' was next, after a visit from Admiral Sir John Treacher, C-in-C Fleet, on 16 February. It started with a full Staff Sea Check on 22 February 1977. Two very intense sea weeks of Basic Operational Sea Training followed, accompanied by a self-conducted ASW work-up in the South-Western Approaches. By 16 March, however, *Hermes* was considered good enough to proceed and set out for Gibraltar and the Med, with RFA's *Olwen* and *Regent* in company. Although only a weekend visit to Gib followed, much sport was played and 140 members of the ship's company attempted the Top of the Rock Race. Although the ship's winning team had the fastest time that half year, it was not quite good enough for the record.

En route for Toulon, the next port of call, Seacat firings were scheduled. They did not last long, however, as the second missile fired shot down the PTA (Pilotless Target Aircraft), despite the operator's attempts to evade the missile. The Toulon visit seems to have included every sport available, from volleyball to sailing, but appeared to serve only to whet the appetites of those on board for sport, as en route

for a Self Maintenance Period in Malta, an Intership Sports Day was organised on Sunday 3 April. Helicopters of 845 and 814 flew in competitors from HM ships *Glamorgan* and *Hermione*, and RFA's *Olwen* and *Regent*, who were in company. The day commenced with a fancy dress parade *extraordinaire*. FOCAS, Rear Admiral W D M Staveley, awarded the prize in the end to a particularly impressive Stores Department panto horse, although other competitors argued that this was only so that he would not be forced to ride the panto horse around the flight deck. Over 400 competitors then indulged in a variety of 'silly games', ranging from swinging across 'bottomless chasms' on ropes, to throwing tennis balls in buckets. The Royal Marines team eventually were declared the winners.

Over 160 people took advantage whilst in Malta of expeds organised to Ta Doiega Camp on Gozo, and Ghain Tuffieha, while many flew out wives and girlfriends for the Easter break.

Exercising off Malta on 20–22 April 1977, the new First Sea Lord (Admiral Sir Terence Lewin, her ex-Captain), visited the ship. Building on the success of the pre-Malta activities, it was decided to hold a horse racing evening in the hangar in honour of the occasion, followed by a fancy dress and kite-flying competition on the next day, Saturday 22 April. Ascot hats were worn for the horse racing, whilst in the fancy dress Admiral Lewin found himself outranked by no less than the Admiral of the World (Leading Steward P L Griffiths). The kite-flyers did not fare so well as, despite the best efforts of the Captain, Navigator and Met officer, wind could not be found. 41 Commando were also aboard when the ship sailed from Malta and the other capability of the ship, Amphibious Assault, was exercised before *Hermes* called at Naples to prepare for the major NATO exercise, Dawn Patrol 77. Tours to Vesuvius, Pompeii and Rome were organised. FOCAS reembarked and the ship sailed to conduct a preexercise work-up, code-named Determined Defenders, in the Tyrrhenian Sea. Exercise Dawn Patrol was marked for the ship by the high levels of submarine and fast patrol boat activity. This ensured intense flying and high alert states for both Sea King and Wessex 5. At 'Endex', the ship rapidly donned its other 'brown' hat, and recovered HQ3 Commando Brigade and its Marines from their temporary camp site at Deciamanu in Sardinia. The ship rapidly filled up with landrovers, trailers, and numerous suspicious-looking jerrycans said to hold water, but believed to contain a Sardinian wine. With the addition of some private cars at Gibraltar, the flight deck more resembled a car park on the homeward trip for AMP and Easter leave. Squadrons disembarked, and all set about getting the ship ready for the Queen's Silver Jubilee review of the Fleet.

Hermes sailed on 17 June, taking sons of crew members on passage to Torbay. There, Torquay and Tiverton were invited to a ship open to visitors on successive days, while final preparations for Spithead were completed. Pomp and ceremony were unrestrained on the occasion of the parade of the Fleet before their Lord High Admiral, plus of course the Duke of Edinburgh and the Prince of Wales, both of whom had held operational command at sea. Pride of place in the line was grudgingly given to 'big sister', HMS *Ark Royal*, with Admiral Sir Henry Leach, CINC Fleet, embarked. *Hermes* was however second in line, flying the Flag of Rear Admiral W D M Staveley, then Flag Officer Carriers and Amphibious Ships. Over 175 ships were present at the review, including 46 RN warships of frigate size or above, 15 submarines and 20 foreign warships from 18 Commonwealth, NATO, EEC and CENTO nations. 150 Fleet Air Arm aircraft were scheduled to complete a flypast, but the majesty of the occasion was not matched by the weather, and on the day only the rotary wing aircraft were able to make the flypast. All but one of the previous Captains of *Hermes* were on board for the actual review on Tuesday 28 June, when Her Majesty the Queen, in HM Yacht *Britannia*, preceded by THV *Patricia* (with Elder Brethren of Trinity House embarked), and followed by HMS *Birmingham* (with Admiralty Board embarked) and RFA *Engadine* (with press embarked) reviewed the Fleet. The following day, *Hermes* followed *Ark Royal* past the Chief of Defence Staff, Admiral of the Fleet Sir Edward Ashmore GCB DSC, and headed for Plymouth to pick up 42 Commando. A fast passage through the Irish Sea preceded a savage assault on the Kyle of Lochalsh in Exercise Forest Venture, and ASW activity in Exercise Highwood in the northeast Atlantic. 40 Commando then joined for the second half of Forest Venture, a swift airdrop onto Dartmoor being made for the commando to find the difficult way back to their barracks at Plymouth. Families joined for the passage up harbour, as *Hermes* returned to Devonport for summer leave and maintenance.

After an extremely busy period over Navy Days, the ship joined *Antrim* and *Kent*, three frigates and two RFAs, for a working passage to Bermuda. Hurricane 'Clara' prevented the ship from entering initially, and it must have been galling to sit five miles to the north-west of the island watching the remainder of the task group berth safely inside the harbour at HMS *Malabar*. Luckily the weather relented and permitted shore leave for the last two days, before two brief visits were made to Mayport and Norfolk, Virginia, interspersed with USMC Harrier operations off Cherry Point USMC Base. The sight of four giant USN carriers, rows of nuclear submarines and lines of frigates and destroyers at Norfolk Naval Base served as a salutary lesson to many of the size and power of the US Navy.

Some of the US ships then joined *Hermes* for Exercise Combined Effort and Ocean Safari, back across the Atlantic — broken again by a visit to Lisbon where the ship had to anchor in the Tagus. After returning to Portsmouth, an informal visit was paid to Copenhagen in November, before leave and maintenance in Devonport rounded off another busy year for the ship. It had been a year in which over 48,000 miles were steamed in nearly 3,400 hours underway.

When *Hermes* sailed from Devonport on 17 January 1978, it was to be her last commission as a dedicated ASW carrier. After a refit at the end of 1979, she was to take Sea Harriers and be fitted with a 'ski jump' ramp on the bow, to improve weapon loads on take-off. 814 Squadron, up-rated with nine Sea King Mk 2 aircraft, and over 200 officers and ratings re-embarked to 'take on' HMS *Conquerer* in the Western Approaches. In the first two weeks away, the ship had three 'sets' of divisions, including FOCAS' Harbour Inspection in Gibraltar. In addition to Exercise Springtrain, FOCAS conducted his Sea Inspection, when Damage Control, tow astern and liferaft stations went on unabated. HM Submarine *Churchill* became *Hermes*' next opponent off Bermuda, preparing for Caribbean waters in Exercise Safe Pass. A visit to Mayport, rapidly becoming a second home for the ship, for a three-week AMP in March/April, enabled many to visit Disneyworld in Florida. With sunshine, beaches, and very friendly 'natives', it proved again an outstanding success.

The ship returned to Bermuda, where Captain D C Jenkins relieved Captain Fitch in command, before crossing the Atlantic in company with STANAVFORLANT (the Standing Naval Force Atlantic) and Exercise Open Gate. A brief 'rabbit' run in Gibraltar, and it was home for Easter and summer leave, plus June in dry dock. The ship then went into intensive work-up for Amphibious Exercises with 40 Commando, airlifting them on 24 August from Staddon Heights, for Exercise Noon Whisper at Castle-

Martin Ranges. It was at this time that aircraft No. 717 of 814 Squadron suffered the loss of her main gearbox oil, due to a mechanical failure. A controlled water landing near Lundy Island in the Bristol Channel followed, and the sea boat hull of the Sea King proved its worth! The helicopter was recovered, somewhat soggy, by the ship's team who had only exercised the procedure four days earlier. All crew and passengers on board were safe, not even getting their feet wet.

After Noon Whisper, parts of 819 and 826 Squadrons, and 'K' Flight of RM Commando were embarked, so that the ship sailed for Den Helder with 24 aircraft on board. The whole team were put at full stretch in the combined ASW/Amphibious Exercise Northern Wedding, which took the ship up to the Hebrides, half-way to Iceland, and across to southern Norway. 'Eight on, eight off' took on a different meaning in the cold, and up to six inches of snow fell on the flight deck one day between 0430 and 0600. It had to be moved by 0800, to allow the ship to go to flying stations. A visit to Copenhagen followed. The ship may have visited there before, but not with the Danish models who came on board — this time for a fashion show as part of a British Week promotion! 40 Commando were transported back from Arendal, forcing the ship to go to overload conditions. The September visit was the last to Devonport, as a proper 'Guzz' ship, transferring allegiance to Portsmouth on completion.

Exercise Octeval, a visit to Hamburg, and Harrier trials in the Moray Firth rounded off the year. Once again the deck echoed to the sound of fixed wing jets, and elder brethren of the carrier fraternity reminisced about the 'good old days' of fixed wing flying. The tears they shed however were probably not so much from nostalgia, as from the quantities of unburnt Avcat pushed out by the aircraft.

Christmas was spent getting to grips with the new base port of Portsmouth, but the New Year saw *Hermes* back at sea for COST (Continuation Operational Sea Training) with old friends at Portland. NATO Exercise Testgate followed in the Gib areas, before embarking Flag Officer Third Flotilla (the new title for FOCAS) and his band, before heading for Naples and Athens. Banyans in extinct volcanic craters were held in Naples, and in the Greek mountains from Athens. There was a difficult exit from Piraeus, when a merchantman tried to cut across *Hermes'* bows. A swiftly-executed 'full astern' averted disaster, and apparently earned the MEO a bottle of wine from the Captain. *Hermes* was diverted on her return to Gib to the Soviet anchorage of Sollum, to inspect the Soviet fleet, which included the new carriers *Minsk* and *Kiev*. *Hermes* took her pictures of the Soviets, and the Soviets took pictures of *Hermes*, even deliberately dropping one Red Star Lapel Badge

on the flight deck after a close pass by a Hormone helicopter. Dartmouth officers under training had been on board since January and were landed at Falmouth before the ship moved to Trondheim for Exercise Cold Winter — with Commodore Amphibious Warfare embarked. A terribly expensive and slippery run ashore in Narvik completed the exercise, and vast numbers of Marine commandos, aircraft vehicles and chacons were packed on board for the return passage to the UK. One fork lift truck fell off the vehicle brow as it was moving on board, finishing up on its side on the jetty. Fortunately, a Norwegian crawler crane and driver were on hand and retrieved the situation by lifting a very tired, bent, but still workable fork lift truck on to the flight deck.

It was on the way back from Narvik that it was discovered which of the deck link plates weren't up to standard, and also that unlashed chacons (large equipment containers) make very good battering-rams. It was unfortunate that the shortwheel-based landrovers, parked astern of the chacons, took the brunt of the rampage, and became *very* shortwheel-based landrovers indeed! The men and what was left of the equipment after the heavy passage, were disembarked in Plymouth on 27/28 March, before taking leave and maintenance in Portsmouth. The bad weather persisted even here, and the plan for a families' up-harbour trip had to be cancelled.

Alongside in Portsmouth, preparations were made for the Westlant deployment, before slipping out on 31 May, heading south into the sun. 814 and 824 Squadrons were embarked for Exercise Jolly Roger. A quick visit to both Gibraltar and Villefranche followed — banyans on beaches where swimmers wore less than usual seemed to form the major attraction. Exercise Highwood served to refocus attention on work, as well as fleet trials with HMS *Lowestoft*. Elements of 819 and 845 Squadrons were embarked off Falmouth on 28 June 1979. Rear Admiral D J Halifax, FOF1, flew his flag on board for Exercise Highwood, leaving the ship in the Firth of Forth on 13 July. Passage was made via the western isles of Scotland and the Portland and Plymouth exercise areas, out to Mayport again. Exercise Mayflower being conducted crossing the Atlantic included a visit by CINC Fleet (Admiral Sir James Eberle). Though this involved 42 days at sea, the undoubted highlight was the day of the Herbert-on-the-Dimmock Grand Village Fête. This event, staged by Air/AED Fun Enterprises Limited, was billed as occurring on Herbday, 23 July 1979, in the best-known village in Hermland, Herbert-on-the-Dimmock. This was a charming and unspoilt village of 1,700 souls, surrounded by a large salt water lake. The village had strong nautical ties, being the home of one Herbert and one Dimmock, sailors of Nelson's ilk, who had settled there. Many dazzling attractions were to be seen, including a performance by the 'Ashby de la Zouch Rutting and Strutting Ethnic DMS Formation Team', and a fancy dress contest, won by three able seamen dressed as 'Sir Ivor Biggun and the two Zulus'. There was a beauty competition, jumble sale and, with a performance by the 'Piddle-Him Tried village band', ensured a marvellous day. Rear Admiral P M Herbert, FOF3, opened the fête, with a naughty film actress, (Miss B Yankemoff), and at the end of the day £760 had been raised for the Sailors' Children's Society.

Mayport was as marvellous as ever for crew rest, recreation, hospitality and trips to Disneyworld, with a visit to Norfolk to follow — some intrepid explorers even going on exped to the Blue Ridge Mountains. On the way back across 'the Pond', the ship exercised anti-submarine warfare almost continually, during Exercise United Effort, with the USN in the Western Atlantic, and Ocean Safari with COMASGRU2 (FOF3) in the Eastern Atlantic. Between 11 September and 5 October 1979 over 1,400 flying hours were logged by the aircraft, no mean achievement.

Ocean Safari ended at Bergen, for a brief visit before returning to Portsmouth, again only briefly, before the annual Naval Harrier Trial in the Carmathen Bay area. This time, in addition to the trials' Harrier and a Wessex Mk 2, the ship embarked two Sea Harriers from 700A Squadron for deck familiarisation and training. The prototype 'Blue Fox' radar came on board with the trials aircraft, as did navigation and attack systems for testing at sea, and a massive team of manufacturers' representatives. The trials were a great success, and the ship returned to Portsmouth in high spirits for Christmas leave, before one final deployment, again to the Caribbean and the States, this time in the Dartmouth training role. Captain D J McKenzie relieved Captain Jenkins in command on 10 December 1979.

When Hermes sailed on 15 January 1980 for the unexpected boost of a further deployment, she did so with only one shaft available, consequent to an indiscretion by one of the boilers. Both shafts became available on 17 January to help the ship reach Port of Spain at Trinidad. FOF3 embarked by helo from Caracas after the ship sailed and joined for the visit to Williamsted, Curacao. He stayed for Arubex, a short exercise with the Dutch Marines, and then left while Hermes stopped for a banyan day at the Grand Cayman. A steering gear failure in the Mississippi, on the way up to the next port of call, New Orleans, kept everyone on their toes, but once alongside, the ship joined in the world-famous Mardi Gras. As the visit coincided with the festival, the ship was honoured by an invitation to lead the parade. The Royal Marine Band, with four platoons of sailors, were given a wonderful reception, as they proudly led the colourful procession through enormous crowds. The band's playing of 'The Stars and Stripes' and 'Colonel Bogey' received enthusiastic acclaim. All who participated from the ship are unlikely ever to forget the occasion, or the visit.

More 'hardship' followed, as the ship visited Pensacola, where HRH The Prince Andrew joined for a brief training acquaint, staying from 22 February to 10 March 1980. A marvellous cruise was rounded off by visits to Fort Lauderdale, Florida, and Bermuda. Mount's Bay was reached on the 19th March, where 820 and 846 Squadrons disembarked, before moving on to Plymouth Sound to disembark BRNC Officers Under Training. Customs and families came out to the ship at Spithead on 20 March, entering harbour later that day, and yet another refit commenced on 24 March 1980.

This refit was to enable Hermes to carry the Sea Harrier and involved a fairly significant 'nose job' of surgery, to fit a 12-degree 'ski jump' to the bow. It was to last 13 months — until May 1981. On 4 November 1980 Captain L E Middleton relieved Captain McKenzie in command. At the end of this commission the ship produced a 'Highlights of Hermes' booklet, covering the period 1978–1980, and containing many anecdotes and stories. One of these is reproduced below . . .

A Fairy Story

It was a dark December night with squalls of sleet blowing across the waters of Portsmouth harbour. HMS Hermes stood, cold and dark, alongside the jetty with her boilers shut down and the shoreside power supplies off once again.

Down on 5 Deck, a small figure sat huddled over a tin of flat beer, wrapped in a blanket with only a torch to light part of the bleak and empty messdeck. Suddenly with a clatter, down the ladder came a figure dressed in a short frilly skirt, boots and gaiters with a Chief's cap planted four square on his shaven dome. The figure paused at the foot of the ladder and did a pirouette. The lad gaped in amazement at this apparition. Suddenly the figure spoke. 'Come come na lad, why so glum?'. The lad found his voice, glad of someone to drip to. 'I'm *@''!@*! duty that's what and I can't go to the ship's dance and I loaned all my gear to me oppo and he'll probably mess it up!'

'Never mind', said the apparition, 'I'm your fairy Joss come to get you to the ball.' 'You must be some kind of raving nutter', said the lad in reply. 'Stand up' snapped the fairy Joss baring his teeth. The lad leapt to his feet, spilling his beer and knocking the torch so that it smashed on the deck. 'Damn', said the lad. 'Don't worry' said the Fairy Joss, his voice seeming to echo in the stygian darkness. 'With one wave of my magic armband — let there be light'. And the mess lights sprang into life. There was a thud as the lad's jaw hit the deck. He gazed at the F.J. with a look that would have done credit to a village idiot. The F.J. circled the lad, gazing critically at his greasy overalls, down at heel steaming boots and the once clean blanket, now wet with spilt beer, still draped around his shoulders.

'Mmmmmmmmm,' murmured the Fairy Joss, 'I think we can do something with that'. He waved his gleaming stardust encrusted armband over the lad's head. BANG! With a flash of light there stood the lad transformed. Instead of greasy overalls, he wore a set of faded pre-shrunk denims by Levi. On his feet were a pair of the finest blue and white training shoes money could buy; whilst over his shoulder was draped a real imitation leather overcoat. The lad gave a shout as he gazed down at his attire. 'I can go to the ball'. 'Follow me' said the Fairy Joss, leading him on to the upper deck and on to the jetty. 'Now all that is missing is your own personal fast black'. He gazed around until his eyes spotted a half-empty dockyard gash cart. With one wave of his armband, and a slightly quieter BANG, the gash cart had turned into a gleaming Rolls. 'There' said the Fairy Joss, 'off you go me lad' but remember this. You must be on board by 0745 tomorrow as that is when the spell wears off. Go on, I'll do your duty for you'. He stood beaming down at the lad 'there's just one thing, I can't drive'. 'Holy Crown', said the Fairy Joss, 'Have I got to do everything for you?' He looked around just as a mangy cat emerged from behind a dustbin. BANG, went the armband again, and there was an immaculate chauffeur on his hands and knees peering around the dustbin. 'Move yourself!' said the Fairy Joss to the chauffeur. Slightly bewildered he approached the car and opened the back door for the lad, who entered the luxurious interior like a King. 'Remember, remember' said the Fairy Joss, '0745 it ends'.

With a grating of gears and weaving slightly, the Rolls pulled away 'First time I've ever ridden in a Rolls', said the lad. 'Well hang on', replied the Chauffeur, 'It's the first time I've driven one'.

The lad had a ball at the ball, eventually emerging with a beautiful spacehopper on his arm. He whistled her off to her home on Hayling Island in the Rolls, where he spent an enjoyable night.

He emerged from the door of the house at 0715 in such a hurry that he left one of his shoes behind. He leapt into the Rolls saying, 'Quick, get us back to the ship. I don't want the spell to wear off out here'. 'Neither do I', said the chauffeur, 'I've a date tonight with a hot tabby.' So they sped along, but all in vain, because at 0745 they had only made it to the jetty, when BANG!!! the spell wore off.

'And that, Sir, is how the Captain happened to spot me sitting in a gash cart at the bottom of the gangway, with only one steaming boot on, dressed in overalls with a blanket draped around my shoulders and clutching a screaming tom cat at 0750 yesterday.'

Right **140** *Hermes runners set out for a 'Top of the Rock' race, Gibraltar, March 1977.*

Below *A hangar horse racing evening, 21 April 1977, en route for Malta.*

Left The Admiral of the World (alias Leading Steward P L Griffiths) offers some words of advice to the First Sea Lord, Admiral Sir Terence Lewin, at the horse racing evening, 21 April 1977.

Below The Kite Flying Competition that lacked the wind; 22 April 1977.

Above During Exercise 'Noon Whisper', Sea King No 272 of 814 Squadron 'splashed in' in the Bristol Channel, near Lundy Island, 25 August 1977...but (**below**) was eventually returned on board by a somewhat unorthodox method . . .

Facing, above HM ships **Antrim** and **Kent** join **Hermes** for deployment to Bermuda and the USA, early September 1977.

Facing, below The flight deck has many uses . . .

115

Above and right The 'Ashby de la Zouche Rutting
and Strutting Ethnic DMS Formation Dancing Team'
perform their ancient rituals on Herbday — in Herbert
on the Dimmock.

Facing, above The village of Herbert on the Dimmock,
Hermland, on Herbday, 23 July 1979

Facing, below The fancy dress of that day: Sir Ivor
Biggun and the two Zulus

*Two faces of the Royal Marine Band: (**left**) they beat retreat in the hangar for assembled dignitaries, whilst (**above**) they show their musical skills at a traditional band concert for the Ship's Company at sea.*

Facing, above *While at sea, on 27 July 1979, a reunion dinner was held for 30 Ex field gun crew members serving on board. Guests of honour were FOF 3, then Rear Admiral P G M Herbert, and the captain, Captain D C Jenkin.*

Facing, below *The Americans salute the arrival of* **Hermes** *at Mayport, her 'second home', 30 July 1979.*

An 820 Squadron aircraft conducting a winching exercise offers a startlingly different view of the flight deck.

814 pilots and observers listen to a pre-launch briefing in No 1 Briefing Room, 1979.

Harrier trials in Carmarthen Bay, October 1979, with a two-seat test aircraft just recovered on deck.

The same aircraft accelerates for a short take-off, with another Harrier in the background forward of the island.

Facing, above Almost
back to fixed wing carrier
days. Sea Harriers from
700A Squadron, and Trials
Harriers 'parked' in the
hangar, October 1979.

Facing, below Arrival
at Curacao February 1980
— in the Dartmouth
Training Squadron rôle.

A man of many talents,
FCPO Cook Hogg running
the banyan in the Grand
Cayman Islands 9 February
1980.

February 1980 — on
board with a sample of the
day's cooking.

Overleaf A visit to
remember! **Hermes** visits
New Orleans for Mardi
Gras 13 to 20 February
1980, and leads the parade
in style.

8

Harrier strike carrier
1981 to 1982

Hermes was non-operational from 24 March 1980 to re-dedication on 5 June 1981, whilst undergoing refit at Portsmouth. In addition to the striking visual feature of the 12-degree launching ramp 'ski jump' fitted to the bow for Sea Harrier operations, the ship was equipped with the most up-to-date Command, Control and Communications facilities. This would enable her to assume the duties of Anti-Submarine Warfare Control Ship for a major NATO Commander at sea.

In her primary role, the ship would carry a squadron of Sea King helicopters capable of both active and passive sonar operations, with the Sea Harrier squadron being borne to counter the long range air and surface threat. The ship however retained the ability to operate as a commando carrier!

Prior to rededication, *Hermes* proceeded to sea on 12 May for sea acceptance trials, under her new Commanding Officer, Captain Middleton. Ten days were spent in the Portsmouth, Portland and Plymouth areas, before a full power trial on the way back to Portsmouth. Final defect rectification then continued until an impressive galaxy of talent descended on the ship for the rededication, including a Sea Harrier from 800 Squadron as the prime display star. The Chief of Defence Staff, Admiral of the Fleet, Sir Terence Lewin, honoured the ship again with his presence, and the Commander-in-Chief Fleet, Flag Officer Third Flotilla, Flag Officer Portsmouth and Major General Royal Marine Commando Forces also attended. Also represented were the organisations affiliated to the ship, The Lady Mayor of Tiverton, TS *Hermes* Sea Cadet Corps, Blundells School and the Worshipful Company of Coachmakers and Harnessworkers from London, the ship's affiliated guild.

The remainder of June was spent with more serious thoughts in mind, off Portland. *Hermes* degaussed, noise ranged, Staff Sea checked, and fought the Thursday War, as the new ship's company settled down. July saw the first major Harrier trials, as 800 Squadron flew extensively by day and by night in the Plymouth areas, but time was found to have a Families Day on 24 July, before some pre-deployment summer leave in August.

Hermes was the prime attraction at Portsmouth for the 1981 Navy Days. By now she was the largest ship in the fleet, and thousands crowded on board for the day; she provided a grandstand position on the flight deck for the flying displays, with the ship even developing a small list to the outboard side from the weight of the crowds! Much work had been done in organising a specially-formed unit of 130 Royal Marines, 'E' Company 41 Commando, for embarkation on the Westlant deployment which was to follow. This was primarily for *Hermes* to operate with the USN, but carrying capacity was available, and the Royal Marines were able to deploy with the ship to Camp Le Jeune US Marine Corps, where they were able to train alongside their United States colleagues. To support them in the airborne assault role, the ship embarked two Sea King Mk 4 Commando helicopters and two Wessex Mk 5s. The carrier's own group (CAG) consisted of 800 NAS with five Sea Harriers and the seven Sea King Mk 2/M5 5 of 812 Squadron.

Sailing on 2 September 1981, the ship paused in its dash States-side, at Rockall. There the ship's RM detachment hoisted a new Union Jack on the summit, to reassert sovereignty. South-west of Iceland, a mini war was declared with the USS *Forrestal* Task Group, before meeting up for passage south to Florida. Although the weather was marginal for flying, it was a significant triumph when the Sea Harriers from the ship found the giant US aircraft carrier and carried out dummy attacks before the US Air Wing could locate the *Hermes* group.

In company with the Americans, exchanges of personnel became a daily occurrence, with 'Zippo' lighters being exchanged for baseball bats, but it was remarked upon how the US Navy always arrived on board *Hermes* every day just before the bar opened.

By 15 September the ship was off Louisiana and disembarked 'E' Company for its training at Camp Le Jeune. It also launched Sea Harriers to defend the ship against A7 Corsair attacks from US Naval Station Cecil Field, who were attacking the ship's splash target. Air battles ensued everywhere, as a prelude to the disembarked time 800 were to have at Cecil Field for the next five weeks, while *Hermes* carried out a Contractor Assisted Maintenance Period (CAMP) at Mayport. 826, 845 and 846 also disembarked to US NAS Jacksonville for continuation flying. One significant milestone was achieved when *Hermes* became the first carrier ever to launch and recover fixed wing aircraft alongside in the naval base.

Whilst ashore, the squadrons were still kept busy flying. 800 sent two Sea Harriers to Pratt and Witneys at West Palm Beach, where they performed for 8,000 spectators in an excellent public relations exercise — even if those nearest the aircraft did get wet as they hovered over an alligator swamp! 826 Squadron detached two aircraft for two weeks of Stingray torpedo trials with HMS *Spartan* in the Bahamas and one aircraft of 845 had to ditch south of Savannah. Crew and passengers were safe, if a little damp from the dunking.

On 20 October, farewells having been made, *Hermes* left Mayport for onward passage to Norfolk, Virginia. Most of the air group were re-embarked, and a USMC AV8A Harrier joined for ski jump evaluation trials. 846 Squadron and 'Echo' Company Royal Marines rejoined at Norfolk, and shortly after leaving the port, Vice Admiral John Cox, FOF3, hoisted his flag on board. He joined from the USS *Dwight D Eisenhower* for Readex 1/82, an exercise involving *Hermes* operating with two USN Carrier Battle Groups, headed separately by USS *John F Kennedy* and *Eisenhower*. 826 carried out an ASW exercise against USN nuclear submarines, while 800 carried out intercept and attack exercises with American air and surface units.

During this three-week period 845 and 846 disembarked, together with 'Echo' Company, to Beef Island, Tortola, in the British Virgin Islands. After the exercise, the ship's company had an opportunity for a banyan on the island of Virgin Gorda. Un-

fortunately, after landing, wind and sea suddenly increased, and recovery of the stranded banyaners had to be by 'Hermairways', using helicopters from 845, 846 and 826 and 'Resource' Flight. Suitably restored, though, the ship returned to the fray of Readex 1/82 for a further week — before a four-day visit to Bermuda en route for the UK. In the sunshine, 'display fever' was rife, and the Harriers had to hover and perform for the governors of Virgin Gorda, Tortola and Bermuda. The pilots said they enjoyed Tortola most, for the high-speed approach, concluding by hovering in Roadtown Bay, in front of the governor's residence.

The warm weather disappeared for the return passage, as the ship went through a force 12 hurricane. Pitch House Jetty was reached on 3 December, with squadrons disembarked, and Christmas for most on board was spent at home. The New Year commenced with anti-submarine exercises in the South Western Approaches with HMS *Invincible*, RFA *Olmeda* and the submarines *Odin* and *Onyx* for which, not only 800 and 826 Squadrons came, but also 814 and 845. A brief visit to Lisbon, from 5 to 10 February 1982 followed, before a role change back to Amphibious with 40 Commando, exercising off the Mevagissey and Falmouth areas.

Happily unaware of the gathering tension in the South Atlantic, but immensely useful in the event, training for active operations continued in March. the normal peacetime activity of the service. Anti-submarine operations with HMS *Spartan* and *Lowestoft* in the South Western Approaches, and Anti Air Exercises with HM ships *Coventry*, *Glamorgan*, *Antrim* and *Ariadne* were carried out. March 19 saw *Hermes* arrive at Portsmouth for a Dockyard Assisted Maintenance Period, from which she was to sail to the South Atlantic.

The 'new look' **Hermes** *— after refit and the 'nose job'*

Left *Admiral of the Fleet Sir Terence Lewin, Chief of Defence Staff, and Lady Lewin, being greeted by Captain Middleton as they arrive on board for the Rededication Service; 5 June 1981.*

Below *Sir Terence Lewin takes the salute, with a Sea Harrier taking pride of place on the after lift.*

Right Preparing to land and reassert sovereignty on Rockall, 5 September 1981.

Below Navy Days at Portsmouth, as the crowds gather on the flight deck to watch the flying display. No wonder the ship developed a list!

9

The Falklands campaign
April to July 1982

At the end of March 1982 *Hermes* was quietly settling into a DAMP (Dockyard Assisted Maintenance Period) in Portsmouth Dockyard. Her squadrons were ashore, as were many of her ship's company — on leave. Scaffolding clad the island, to the top of the mast, and major surgery was being undertaken below. A normal 'quote' for being rushed to sea would have been three weeks; in the event the ship was given 72 hours, and achieved it. The unique experience of sailing to war provided arguably the most intense and extraordinary activity seen in the Royal Navy since the outbreak of the Second World War.

The magnitude of the task, with recall of the ship's company and the logistic effort to store and prepare for war in such a short time still defies the imagination. Bewildering to the onlooker, and exhilarating to the participant, it was an experience few who encountered it will ever forget.

Hermes' somewhat modest Air Group was immediately brought up to wartime strength, and the ship sailed with 800 and 899 Harrier Squadrons, 826 Sea King ASW Squadron and 846 Sea King Commando Squadron embarked, as well as 'A' Company of 40 Commando Royal Marines. A somewhat unimaginative or laconic ship's log entry for 5 April 1982 records the departure from Portsmouth with the words 'large crowds wave ship off'. In fact the largest fleet Britain had put to sea for many decades sailed to an incredible display of public support, with thousands crowding their way into Portsmouth to make their farewells to their men and the ships, only three days after the invasion of British sovereign territory by Argentina.

The ship immediately commenced the serious business of shaking off peacetime concepts and procedures and, waiting in the South Western Approaches for the remainder of the Task Force to join, carried out an intensive series of flying operations, embarking last minute stores; she then made passage for Ascension Island. The equator was passed on 15 April, and a rendezvous made with *Glamorgan*, for Rear Admiral 'Sandy' Woodward, Flag Officer First Flotilla, to embark — *Hermes* had become Flagship for the campaign.

Ascension was reached on 16 April, and CINC-FLEET visited on 17 April for briefings, before the ship sailed for the Total Exclusion Zone (TEZ) on 18 April, in company with *Invincible, Glamorgan, Broadsword, Alacrity, Yarmouth* and *Resource*. Surveillance by an Argentinian 707 aircraft started on 21/22 April, as the ship continued working up, and tragically a Sea King 4 was lost during a night vertical replenishment in bad visibility on 23 April. All were recovered, except Petty Officer Aircrewman Ben Casey, the ship's first casualty of the campaign.

On 25 April *Antrim* led the forces who recaptured South Georgia, and crippled the submarine *Santa Fé*, caught on the surface, and on 1 May *Hermes* entered the TEZ, launching a 12 Sea Harrier strike on Port Stanley and Goose Green, in conjunction with the dawn RAF Vulcan bomber attack. As recorded at the time ('I counted them out, and I counted them back'), all aircraft returned safely, but the tempo increased sharply with the torpedo attack and sinking of the *Belgrano* by *Conqueror* on 2 May 1982. By now all aboard were not allowed to sleep below the water line, which led to some fairly crowded passageways, littered with sleeping bodies working a full Defence Watch routine around the clock.

On 3 May Sea Skua missiles were used for the first time in the Falklands and successfully sank one patrol boat and damaged another. But on 4 May the Task Force suffered its first losses. Three Sea Harriers from 800 Squadron attacked Puccaras and gun emplacements at Goose Green, and Lieutenant Nick Taylor from the ship was shot down and killed. It was the first Harrier loss due to enemy action. It was also the day HMS *Sheffield* was attacked by two low flying Super Etendards of the Argentine Navy whilst on forward radar picket duty about 60 miles southeast of the Falklands. Two Exocet missiles were fired, one of which hit *Sheffield* amidships on the starboard side. Casualties were taken and firemain pressure lost. After about 4½ hours the crew abandoned ship, and many injured were taken to *Hermes. Arrow* performed prodigious feats in assisting, but *Sheffield*, under tow by *Yarmouth*, sank on 10 May in heavy seas.

Helicopters of 846 Squadron were used, at this time, on many missions of great daring and danger, with Special Forces. One however was lost, with heavy casualties, during a transfer operation on 19 May, caused by birdstrike at a critical moment. Aircraft reinforcements were taken, in the nick of time, on 18 May, when four Sea Harrier and five RAF Harrier GR3 from 1(F) Squadron RAF Wittering were embarked from the ill-fated merchantman *Atlantic Conveyor*.

An amphibious assault at San Carlos Bay on 21 May, and hard fighting followed, with *Hermes* providing air cover (Combat Air Patrol — CAP) and ground attack missions. Approximately 15 enemy aircraft were destroyed that day, while over 3,000 troops and over 1,000 tons of equipment were successfully landed. HMS *Ardent* was lost, but the force was ashore, and numbers had risen to over 5,000 men ashore by the following morning. For the next few weeks, all efforts by Sea Harriers were devoted to protecting the ships in and around the San Carlos waters, while the GR3 Harriers assisted with ground attack. Sea Harriers on CAP patrolled the outer layers of defences, and any enemy aircraft who broke through them met the second layer of defence, two warships off the entrance to Falkland Sound, in what was called the 'missile trap' — normally a Type 42 with Sea Dart and a Type 22 with Sea Wolf missiles. Three or four warships then patrolled inside the entrance to the sound in what was called the 'gun line', throwing up a wall of fire at any penetrating aircraft. Lastly, in the anchorage area itself, nicknamed 'bomb alley', ships at anchor fired Sea Cat missiles, hand launched Blowpipe missiles, machine guns and small arms, while the army's Rapier anti-aircraft batteries fired missiles from the hillsides surrounding the shore. The end of May saw further losses, both to the ship and the Task Force. Lieutenant Commander 'Gordy' Batt's Sea Harrier blew up just after launch for a night bombing raid on Port Stanley on 23 May; HMS *Antelope* was lost on 24 May when an unexploded bomb detonated while a disposal attempt was in progress; HMS *Coventry* was lost on 'missile trap' duties on 25 May; and the *Atlantic Conveyor* was lost the same day to an Exocet attack — meant for *Hermes*. On 26 May *Bristol* and five frigates joined the Task Group, just before British forces began their move out of the beachhead. Just preceding the Darwin/Goose Green attack by 2 Para, for which *Hermes* provided GR3s in support, a GR3 was lost to ground fire, but the pilot managed to eject. A further GR3 was lost, following a ground attack mission on Mount Kent on 30 May, but the pilot ejected into the sea and was picked up.

All this time, unsung but enormously busy, was 826 Squadron, employed on anti-submarine duties. The threat from the two Argentinian Navy German-built submarines, and a sister ship of the *Santa Fé*, was considerable, and with only nine aircraft and 15 aircrews, 826 NAS kept three aircraft airborne around the clock for two months, a magnificent achievement. Two aircraft were lost to the elements, but on both occasions crews were quickly located and happily recovered, cold but otherwise none the worse for their experiences. Both crews were airborne again within 36 hours in replacement aircraft.

A notable feat at the time was the ferry flight of two further GR3s from Ascension, to replace battle losses. This flight, of some 3,500 miles in 7½ hours with five air-to-air refuellings, flown entirely over the sea in a single-seat, single-engine aircraft, was a vivid demonstration of the remarkable Harrier performance. It also spoke volumes for the ability of the pilot to sit with his legs crossed!

Early June brought further tragedy to the Task Force, with the bombing of the Royal Fleet Auxiliaries *Sir Galahad* and *Sir Tristram*, with very heavy casualties. The balance was only slightly redressed when two patrolling Sea Harriers from *Hermes* shot down four Mirages over Choiseul Sound.

British forces continued their pincer movement on Port Stanley and took the high ground overlooking the capital in fierce fighting on 11/12 June. Paveway laser-guided bombs were deployed on GR3 aircraft for the first time, with some success, but further opportunity to develop experience was not forthcoming with the surrender of General Menendes and a ceasefire on 14 June. A Paveway attack from *Hermes* on Argentine headquarters on Sapper Hill was only ten minutes from execution when the announcement was made, and the aircraft called off.

The remainder of June was spent operating in the eastern part of the Exclusion Zone, providing air cover for ground forces and organising logistic support, before Rear Admiral (later Vice Admiral) Reffell, Flag Officer Third Flotilla, and his staff embarked for briefings on 1 July 1982. He assumed command of the Task Group that day and moved to *Invincible* on 2 July. On 3 July a full Air Group Flypast took place over Port Stanley, before *Hermes* detached to return to the UK, finally falling out from Defence Watches on 7 July — to everyone's relief. By 20 July *Hermes* was making passage up the Channel and conducted a steam past with *Illustrious*, proceeding to the Falklands to relieve *Invincible*. The ship anchored overnight in Sandown Bay to prepare for the events of the next day, when the Prime Minister, accompanied by Admiral of the Fleet (now the Lord) Lewin, Chief of Defence Staff, visited *Hermes*. To great rejoicing and a tumultuous welcome, *Hermes* entered Portsmouth safe and sound on 21 July 1982 — a day that will long be remembered by her ship's company, their families, the general public (who turned out in their thousands) and television viewers around the world.

Left *Sea Harriers land on* **Hermes** *for the Falklands campaign. The urgency is highlighted by the fact that scaffolding still clads the island. Normally, under peacetime regulations, this is a bar to flying operations.*

Below *Frenetic preparations: 'A' Company of 40 Commando, who were to take passage with the ship, embark ammunition via the after lift to the magazines below.*

Right Defence Secretary John Nott,
escorted by Captain Middleton, tours
the ship on 4 April 1982, the day before
the ship deployed to the South Atlantic.

Below Crowds fill the Round Tower
and surrounding areas of Old Portsmouth
— or, as the ship's log put it, 'Large
crowds wave ship off'; 5 April 1982.

Facing, above and below Two views of
Hermes leaving Portsmouth for the
South Atlantic, augmented to war
strength with 12 Harriers and 18
Sea King helicopters — a formidable
sight.

Right *Stores continue to be delivered as the Task Force moves down Channel. Here an RAF Chinook followed by Sea King helicopters bring on board equipment needed for the coming campaign.*

Below *Men of 'A' Company 40 Commando Royal Marines keep their eye in as they work out on the flight deck; 7 April 1982.*

Above 14 April 1982: the ship is overflown by a Soviet Bear 'D', but receives close attention from a Sea Harrier.

15 April 1982: war or no war, the due ceremonies of crossing the line are observed by Neptune's court.

Left 15 April 1982: rendezvous with **Glamorgan** and Flag Officer First Flotilla; Rear Admiral J 'Sandy' Woodward and staff embark. **Hermes** becomes Flagship of the Task Group for the Falklands campaign. Here the battle group commander is greeted by the captain.

Below, left Easter Monday, 17 April 1982: Captain Lyn Middleton greets his son, Sub-Lieutenant Ray Middleton, a Lynx pilot with the Task Force; he had just flown in with stores.

Below, right Before battle was joined there was still time for fun. Easter Sunday, 18 April 1982, proved to be such a day, with a contestant in the 'Mexican Moustache Growing Competition'. Petty Officer Hudson, as an 'Argentinian spy', sports a neat moustache, plus a bandolier of 30 mm canon shells and a fat cigar.

Facing A dramatic dawn shot, as aircraft are readied on deck for combat air patrol.

The flight deck alive with aircraft operations during the campaign, busier than at any stage in its previous 23 years. Yet the safety records maintained showed a clean sheet on deck — despite the massive quantities of live ordnance handled (see photo below) — an impressive achievement speaking volumes for the professionalism of the flight deck team.

The weather was frequently less than kind. The results of a recent torrential down-pour are clearly visible during a brief lull which enabled this picture to be taken.

***Hermes** refuels her 'Goalkeeper' escort, the Sea Wolf missile-armed **HMS Broadsword**. Her job was to use her missile system to defend the High Value Unit (HVU) **Hermes** — she was a welcome sight.*

Above A marvellous picture as dawn breaks in the South Atlantic, showing Royal Marine commandos preparing for action, with the hangar full of aircraft.

Facing, above Near disaster — a fully bombed-up GR 3 Harrier suffers engine problems and lands more awkwardly and in a hurry, one wheel missing the flight deck.

Facing, below Immediate assistance is given, the manual way. How many men do you need to lift a Harrier? Never before undertaken 'in the field': the wing is removed to allow an engine change (**right**), to get the Harrier operational again. A marvellous Air Engineering achievement.

Above A poignant moment in the aftermath of conflict: Captain Middleton and the chaplain, the Reverend Roger Devonshire, stand in silent tribute over the grave of Lieutenant Nicholas Taylor, killed in action over Goose Green on 4 May 1982.

Right Captain Middleton greets the Prime Minister, Mrs Margaret Thatcher, as she boards **Hermes** on return to Portsmouth 21 May 1982.

Facing Home at last . . . the nation rejoices at the safe return of her heroes; loved ones crowd the jetty at Portsmouth, 21 May 1982.

142

10

The final phase, CVS/LPH
1982 to 1984

After *Hermes*' return from the South Atlantic, the ship was taken in hand by Portsmouth Dockyard for a period of maintenance and a much-needed new coat of paint. This was the start of a period of considerable change in the ship's company. People who had been due to leave during the spring and early summer of 1982 now did so. Many people who had remained on board because of the campaign were now relieved by people who had expected to join the ship earlier. Captain Middleton handed over command to Captain Dimmock, who had previous appointments to *Hermes* — so his arrival was, in a sense, a re-forming of an existing relationship with the ship. Captain Middleton, already decorated for his leadership of the Fleet Flagship during the Falklands Campaign, was promoted to Rear Admiral and became Assistant Chief of Naval Staff (Operations).

On 19 November *Hermes* resumed her role as Flagship of the South Atlantic Task Force for one final night. Max Hastings of the *Daily Express* newspaper and Lord Matthews of Cunard financed the holding of a Falklands' Task Force Ball in the ship's hangar. This normally stark and functional area was turned into — as one journalist put it — 'a ballroom that would have graced the Ritz'. All the participating ships, units and squadrons of the three armed services were represented, as were the merchant service and the Ministry of Defence civilian staff. A special guest was Selina Scott, the ITN newscaster who had become very popular with the ship's company via the repeats of her broadcasts, shown on the ship's internal television programmes. It was a glittering occasion and a fitting conclusion to a most important episode in the ship's history.

A week later, 75 girls from the Mayflower Corps Girls' Marching and Display Team, from Billericay in Essex, came on board to entertain and tour the ship.

In late November, after 12 weeks in dockyard hands, *Hermes* returned to sea for a shakedown cruise. 845 NAS Wessex and 737 NAS Sea King helicopters and a small number of 800 NAS Sea Harriers embarked, so once again the Air Engineering Department could get to work. The marine engineers were keen to

'flash up' the boilers and tune their engines again, after they had been 'cold' for so many weeks. The first exercise in the Channel was a high-speed trial, to ensure that the 'old lady' could still pick up her skirts and run if asked to do so. She could!

Brest was visited with Rear Admiral Sir John Woodward, the Falklands' Task Force Commander, embarked — causing considerable interest with the French press and television, as was to be expected so soon after operations in the South Atlantic.

Before Christmas leave started, a party of 15 went to visit *Hermes*' affiliated town of Tiverton, Devon, with 'Christmas hampers'. Pensioners who are looked after by the Meals on Wheels service each received a hamper prepared by the ship's catering staff. The hospitals and hospices of Tiverton were given cakes, carols were sung, and all who went from the ship felt they were given a splendid start to their own Christmas by the warmth of the welcome they received.

On 18 January *Hermes* sailed for a period of five weeks away from Portsmouth. The first evolution was a rather unusual one. TV AM, the breakfast TV channel, asked the ship to write the word 'Britain'. They had already used people on the ground, pigeons in Trafalgar Square, and parachutists; now it was to be *Hermes*' turn! What was feared to be a daunting exercise in interpretation of ideas from a plethora of art directors, design consultants, producers and technicians, was soon reduced to a straightforward drill by the power of command of the Mark 1 Gunnery Instructor (GI). TV folk quickly withdrew in the face of devastating professionalism — and the job was completed in an hour.

With the Sea Harriers of 800 Naval Air Squadron and the Sea Kings of 814 embarked, the ship sailed up the west coast of Scotland, through the Pentland Firth and down to Rosyth. Throughout this passage, intensive flying, anti-submarine exercises and damage control testing were carried out. All this effort contributed to the 'work-up' necessary before Exercise Roebuck. The Scottish weather did its worst, and not for the first time, HMS *Cochrane*'s gym was host to over 500 of *Hermes*' ship's company, stranded ashore.

144

Exercise Roebuck involved ships and aircraft for ten days in the seas north of Scotland. British, American, Dutch, Norwegian, German and Canadian ships took part in mountainous seas, appalling weather and poor visibility. When Roebuck was over, Hermes sailed down to Rosyth for a day of evaluation and discussion with the other participants in the exercise; the period included emergency recovery of a Sea King using vast quantities of mattresses!

On 17 February 1983, a cold foggy morning, *Hermes* sailed up the Elbe to Hamburg. The city provided a wealth of different types of entertainment and interest. Many trips had been arranged, including one for a small number to East and West Berlin, as guests of the British Army. An ice hockey match was arranged by the physical training staff, who valiantly tried to turn skaters into hockey players and hockey players into skaters — on board! 814 NAS took the opportunity to host a NATO 'Mini Tiger' meeting whilst in port, and had attenders from Canadian Starfighters and German Alfa Jet and Phantom squadrons who share the Tiger on their crest. Mission target that day was selected as the Reeperbahn, where all are believed to have 'flamed out'! Throughout the five-day visit, the level of interest shown in the ship and the warm regard in which Britain and the Royal Navy are held were most evident. The verdict on board was that Hamburg was a 'good run ashore'.

After a short break, the massive task of re-storing the floating village was undertaken. For three days everything that the ship would need, from crockery to crisps, from needles to netting, and from beer to balaclavas, was loaded. This time Arctic stores of all kinds were needed for the waters off northern Norway, during Exercise Cold Winter, where Royal Marines and their Dutch counterparts (the 'Cloggies') went to exercise defence against an invasion attempt. *Hermes'* role was to provide air support of all types to the ground forces, and to move Dutch and Royal Marines and their vehicles and guns from one area to another. In practice, this meant that the ship nosed down the fjords embarking or disembarking men and equipment by helicopter, before heading out to sea again. The scenery was spectacular; ranges of snow-clad pinnacles, with small chalet villages clustered beneath them. In all, the ship spent two weeks north of the Arctic Circle. At the end of the exercise, 45 Commando Royal Marines re-embarked and were taken south to Arbroath, their base. The ship was crowded with an extra 600 Marines and soldiers, but it had been a year and more since *Hermes* took a commando to the South Atlantic, and it was pleasant to have 'Royal' back on board under such relaxed circumstances. With Sea Harriers, ASW and amphibious helicopters, *Hermes* was shown to be truly multi-aircraft, multi-role.

After Easter leave, *Hermes* sailed for the United States and, except for a long range SAR by 814 to a troubled Panamanian bulk tanker, the passage was reasonably uneventful. New York was exciting and vibrant, even if it did snow as the ship was entering port in a most unseasonable welcome. However, six days in the 'Big Apple', together with a 'Britain Salutes New York' festival, made for a very successful visit.

En route for Mayport, Florida, the ship entertained numerous American government defence and press officials on board, where they enjoyed Sea Harrier and Sea King 'Shopwindow' displays. At Mayport the ship again settled down to a CAMP (Contract Assisted Maintenance Period) and experienced the efficiency and work output of American private industry. Squadrons meanwhile spread their wings over Florida, disembarking to Cecil Field, Jacksonville and Tindall, and participated in NAS Jacksonville's Air Station Day and Boy Scout America Camp 83. Many families joined the ship in superb Florida sunshine, before the ship moved to Norfolk, Virginia, for Exercise United Effort and Exercise Ocean Safari briefings. 800 Squadron took the opportunity to move to NAS Oceana nearby and flew a variety of sorties against opponents including F14, F-5 and A-4, as well as F15s from Langley USAF Base. The squadron re-embarked on 26 May in full view of the holiday-makers on Virginia Beach, to work with the USS *John F Kennedy* in Exercise United Effort.

There are those who held the navigator personally responsible for the next phase of *Hermes* operations and claimed he was unable to find Portsmouth! Returning from nearly three months away, the ship made its way as far as Mount's Bay to disembark 814 NAS and end a remarkably long association between the ship and squadrons stretching over 40 years. But baulking at Portsmouth, the ship went straight for a visit to Gothenburg. 800 NAS disembarked to exercise ashore with the Royal Swedish Air Force from their base at Saterner, exercising with the SAAB Viggen. Magnificent weather brought thousands of visitors on board, and with the superb scenery in the vicinity and traditional Swedish hospitality, Gothenburg was declared another 'really good visit' by the ship's company.

Next the ship re-embarked old friends — No 1 RAF Squadron of GR3 Harriers for Exercise Mallet Blow in the North Sea. Then, you've guessed it, missed Portsmouth again en route to Portland to disembark 800 Squadron. In their place the ship embarked two Wessex of 845 Squadron and returned to Scandinavia, to pay a visit to Oslo, cancelled earlier due to the Falklands crisis — and of course missed Portsmouth for the third occasion. People were now beginning to talk about the navigator! It obviously preyed on his mind as, after Oslo, he made a complete hash of the fourth opportunity to find Portsmouth, and the ship went to Falmouth before some Indian Sea Harriers arrived on board for deck landing practice off Plymouth. Encouraged by all, 'N' made a fifth attempt and found 2,000 families waiting for him in Portsmouth, and so turned straight round and took them back to the Isle of Wight for a last Families Day at sea. It is said that domestic pressures steeled his nerves to make a second, successful entry on the same day, to offer summer leave on 21 July 1983.

By now rumours were abounding of proposals to scrap *Hermes*, the ship having already been mentioned in Australian plans to purchase her in place of *Invincible*, Chilean intentions and Indian plans for a two-carrier force. In a hectic six week spell alongside in Portsmouth, *Hermes* was intent on combining a maintenance period, giving summer leave, role-changing from carrier to amphibious, and Captain Dimmock being relieved by Captain K A Snow. The ship was also invited to host the change of Flag Officers of the Third Flotilla, when Rear Admiral Fitch was to relieve Vice Admiral Reffell. This changeover on board ensured that Vice Admiral Sir Derek Reffell served on board in every rank from midshipman. Also, both admirals were, of course, ex-commanding officers of *Hermes*.

The ship sailed on 13 September 1983, and at Plymouth embarked 40 Commando Royal Marines, together with the 105 mm Light Guns of 79 (Kirkee) Battery Royal Artillery, 180 vehicles and trailers, and all associated stores and ammunition. An amphibious work-up was conducted off the north coast of Cornwall, inserting the complete commando into the Davidstow Training Area. There was one exciting moment when a Wessex V carrying out an emergency running landing, forgot about the Sea King parked in the 'Green' by the island, and its rotor blade sliced neatly through the tail blade of the Sea King. Fortunately, nobody was injured and the Wessex continued to a safe recovery.

Settling down to the amphibious role continued while *Hermes* made her passage to Naples. Many of the sailors and marines had never worked together before, and it was remarkable how well all reacted to the requirement. With almost 2,000 men on board, the ship became quite crowded, and queues for lunch, for NAAFI, or for the showers became the name of the game. It was a constant surprise how cheerful everybody remained.

On arrival in Naples, for Exercise Display Determination briefings, COMAW, Commodore P G F V Dingemans DSO, arrived, as did Brigadier (later Major General) J M C Garrod OBE RM. The visit had also been intended for storing, but as Fleet had managed to find an RFA for *Hermes*, this requirement was happily unnecessary. Despite being at anchor, some shore leave was possible, but for many on board,

however, it was a working visit. The Captain was then able to inform the ship's company of future plans for the ship. These were to keep *Hermes* in commission to the end of the year, before undergoing a period of essential defect maintenance in Devonport, not her base port, from December 1983 to April 1984. She was then to return to Portsmouth and enter PxO (Preservation by Operation), until HMS *Ark Royal* entered service in 1985. The ship was still to be available for operational emergencies, but the manpower was to be run down drastically after return to the UK. It was a decision forced by manpower shortages, particularly of some categories which *Hermes* required in large numbers, and was the alternative to paying off a squadron of frigates. Regret was a major emotion on board, at the premature paying off of a valuable strategic NATO anti-submarine and amphibious asset, which had some number of years of active service available to her.

These future plans for *Hermes* led to the arrival of the drafting team from HMS *Centurion*, who flew out to join the ship, as the sailors were already within normal drafting notice, and swift action was necessary to see if personal preferences could be met for their next draft. By and large the team managed to satisfy most on board, but 'Drafty' always operates under the reality of 'you can't please *all* the people *all* of the time', and given the short notice *and* shortage categories, faced a very difficult, well-nigh impossible task.

The Task Group sailed for Exercise Display Determination 83, knowing that there were diplomatic difficulties between Greece and Turkey yet again, which threatened the exercise. But it was immediately before the Greek landing phase that the ship was told that Greece had unilaterally decided to withdraw from the exercise, claiming 'Turkish intransigence', and *Hermes* was no longer welcome. Some rapid re-planning took place to enable a rehearsal landing off the toe of Italy, before the ship assaulted Saros Bay in Turkey. En route for assault, the ship was invited to host the flag and staff of Flag Officer Third Flotilla, after a serious defect in HMS *Illustrious* necessitated her withdrawal from the exercise. It was fascinating to observe how easily the ship coped. She just seemed to give a little shake and absorb the Flag Officer and his staff, accommodation and facilities appearing like magic. It would be interesting to pose the question of how one of the *Invincible* class carriers would cope with the combination of major assault responsibilities, plus COMAW, plus Commander 3 Commando Brigade, plus FOF3! — suffice it to say *Hermes* rose to the occasion magnificently.

Saros Bay landings were enlivened by the inclement weather, which assisted in putting paid to most plans laid by PR (public relations) wizards. The gluey effect of earth churned up into mud by rain and military activity, tended to take its toll from time to time, and this was no exception — several high-ranking officers not quite presenting the picture of a cool, collected battlefield officer after slipping and falling head first into the mud!

While the ship was at Saros Bay, there was also a complex operation after an accident ashore involving a Wessex V helicopter making the mistake of a down-wind approach. Ground vortex resulted in a severe case of loss of lift, and a fairly impressive 'prang', fortunately without injury. Efforts to borrow a USAF Chinook for the recovery failing, the helo was stripped down and recovered on board by 846 Sea King, an impressive spectacle.

After the exercise, full speed was made for Istanbul, where the ship anchored from 16 to 21 October 1983, in midstream Bosphorous. The pontoon placed to provide berthing for the local boats was tended by a living-in keeper, who kept the gangway staff alert by appearing daily at 0530 to demand hot water for his tea! While the ship anchored, three major Soviet warships passed close by through the deep channel, and all on board had the opportunity to consider, and reconsider, the impressive warships and equipment of modern Soviet maritime power. The importance of the Bosphorous and the size of the 'threat' assumed new significance.

Hermes then sailed to Cyprus, where 40 Commando disembarked to the AKAMAS military training area, and exercised ashore, building up to a most exciting frontal assault by the entire commando.

In the interim period, unhappy Lebanon continued with its conflict. The ship was honoured, yet saddened, when Surgeon Lieutenant Tulloch was asked to accompany Red Cross Serials to Beirut by USAF C130 from Cyprus, to tend and evacuate the American wounded from the suicide bombing of the US Marine Peacekeeping Force headquarters.

Two Portsmouth Dockyard craftsmen will remember this time, as they were flown out to join the ship to rebuild A1 boiler's monolithic wall, and clear an operational defect.

On 28 October the ship anchored off Alexandria for a working visit to the Egyptian Armed Forces. Exercises at sea and ashore in maritime and military tactics followed, though perhaps not at the force level of the US/Egyptian Exercise Bright Star the year before. When looking for an exercise code name, the British suggestion of 'Dull Star' raised the biggest laugh of the day, and from then on relations were most cordial, even if language barriers and differing operational practices did pose some problems from time to time.

While at Alexandria the renowned tour company 'Hermtours' achieved one of its biggest successes. Literally hundreds of sailors and marines went on a variety of all-day coach trips to Cairo. Leaving very early, they travelled by coach down the Nile Delta, with fascinating scenes of whitewashed mud dwellings, without electricity or running water, washing being done by hand in the river, and irrigation by a donkey on the wheel. On arrival at Cairo, most went to the world-famous Cairo Museum, to marvel at the Pharoah's treasures. After haggling in the bazaars and a meal, many attended the English language floodlit *son et lumière* at the pyramids of Giza. As the sonorous tones of Richard Burton rolled over a spellbound audience, the history of these monuments and the Sphinx was unfolded.

After Alexandria, the programme encountered some difficulties. Ship efforts to visit Venice or Trieste foundered for one reason or another, so it was decided to make a more extended visit to Gibraltar. So, via a pyrotechnic extravaganza on 5 November 1983, and a successful assault on the Fleet record for the 100 mile relay race, the ship arrived alongside in Gibraltar on 11 November. This was the first day alongside for two months, and the ship's company and embarked force made the most of it! A successful assault on the Top of the Rock Race record by Sgt Lindsay RM was also made during this visit.

Homeward bound, Indian Sea Harriers embarked for Deck and Combat Air Patrol training in the Plymouth areas. It was good to see them, and especially so when the last landing and launch from *Hermes* was carried out by a Royal Navy officer, Lt Cdr M S Blisset from NAS Yeovilton. 76 (Kirkee) Battery R A left the ship by air at Plymouth, and as the ship moved up channel for the last time with a full complement on board, Admiral Sir William Staveley, Commander-in-Chief Fleet, honoured the ship and her ship's company by joining for the passage, meeting many, and addressing all on board. Flag Officer Third Flotilla, Rear Admiral R G A Fitch, also accompanied the ship on her last passage as, with a large press contingent and a 750-foot-long paying-off pennant, *Hermes* berthed at North West Wall Portsmouth on 22 November 1983.

Within the next seven days the ship had de-ammunitioned, landed all squadron aircraft and personnel, and bid farewell to the men of 40 Commando, off to their new home at Norton Manor Camp Taunton; also, the first of the officers and men had dispersed to new ships and new jobs, to meet the critical manpower needs of the Fleet.

One interesting arrival at this time was a new Assistant Secretary (Personnel) to the Captain, Second Officer Liz Nuttall WRNS. Believed to be the first-ever complement billet appointment of a woman officer to a ship on the Active List, as *Hermes* still was, the necessary Commander-in-Chief approval was given for her to remain on board at sea overnight on several occasions.

Arriving in Devonport on 30 November, with much assistance from HMS *Drake*, final preparations were completed for a grand finale, the 'End of Commission' Ball. All ex-*Hermes* officers had been invited to attend, and no fewer than seven ex-Captains were able to join Captain Snow – including Admiral Sir John Fieldhouse, the First Sea Lord. All involved worked extremely hard to produce a magnificent occasion enjoyed by the hundreds who attended, and in no way did the ship have the appearance or attitude of being about to cease active service. Christmas leave did however see the major exodus of manpower from the ship, and soon only 400 men (and one woman) were left to work with the dockyard. A very reduced contingent paid a final visit to Tiverton on 9 March 1984, to exercise their Freedom rights for the last time, a nostalgic occasion.

Finally, after an excellent Essential Defect Rectification Period alongside in Devonport, *Hermes* sailed on 6 April 1984, on time and within budgeted costings, for final sea trials. With only 400 ship's company on board, some complement enhancement was necessary, but even so there were precious few people for the job, compared with a normal crew of over 1,200. But all went well, and the carrier entered Portsmouth for the last time on the morning of 12 April 1984. It just so happened that whilst undergoing trials her half-sister, the carrier HMS *Bulwark*, was being towed from Portsmouth to a Scottish scrapyard. With sirens moaning a lament, the two carriers passed off the Eddystone Light – one to the scrapyard, the other to Portsmouth.

Within a month, *Hermes* could be seen locked into a Portsmouth Dockyard basin, crew reduced to just over the hundred men needed to keep her in a state of Preservation by Operation. She is available, still, for operational service at short notice, should the Fleet need her, but probably only until HMS *Ark Royal* enters service in 1985. Her future then must be uncertain. Her career, however, has spanned 24 years, covered the globe, and seen her role change from fixed wing to commando carrier to anti-submarine carrier. Thousands of Navy and ex-Navy personnel have served in the ship and regard her with the greatest of pride and affection. 'Happy *Hermes*' was a name coined in the First Commission, back in 1959, and is one which stuck. She has served the Navy and her country well over many years, and deserved to have her story told . . .

Below January 1983: **Hermes** *helps TV AM write the word 'Britain' for our television screens – spelt out 'in sailors'.* **Facing** *Exercise Cold Winter, March 1983, saw* **Hermes** *in multi-role operations as both ASW and amphibious. Weather conditions off Norway, as can be seen, were less than kind. Snow dusts the flight deck, but does not stop flying operations; Exercise Roebuck (***inset***), January 1983 – an emergency recovery, onto mattresses! – of an 814 Squadron Sea King.*

Above **Hermes** *heading out past Drake's Island, Plymouth Sound, with 40 Commando RM embarked, for her final Mediterranean deployment; September 1983.*

Hungry commandos line up for lunch ashore during training in Italy, September 1983 — some lunch queue!

'H' Hour and 'L' Hour approaches at Saros Bay, Turkey, during Exercise Display Determination 83. Hermes' LCVPs swing past the ship, laden with 40 Commando Royal Marines, as the helicopters load up on deck; October 1983.

An 846 Squadron Sea King 4 recovers the disabled 845 Squadron Wessex V at Saros Bay, Turkey. Tail plane, rotor head and engine have been removed to lighten the lift. The tie lines hanging below carry weighted bags for airborne stability.

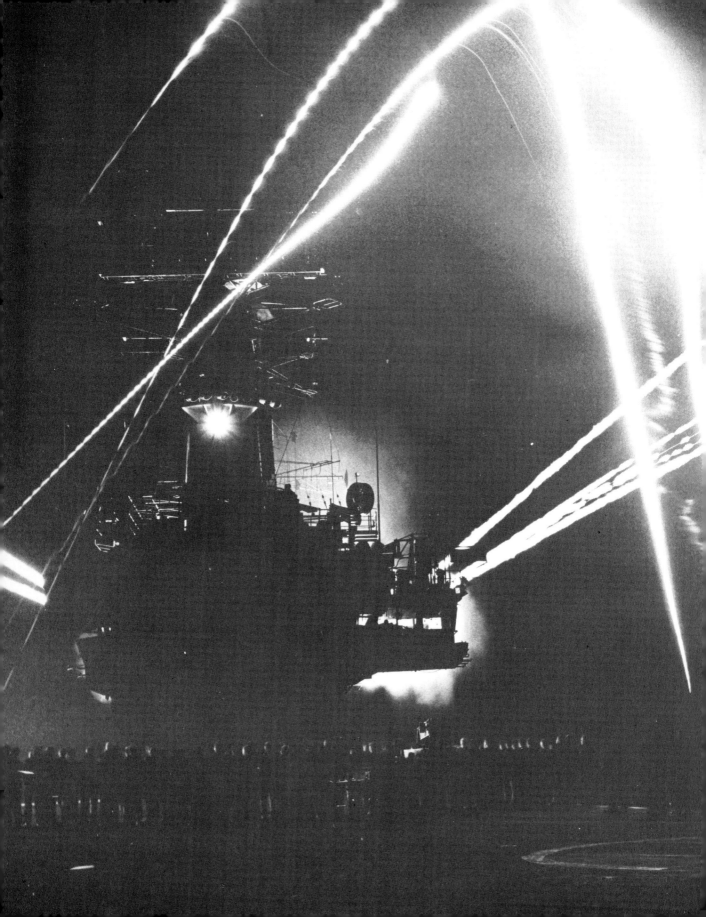

Facing Guy Fawkes night, 5 November 1983, and a fireworks display as 3-inch rockets are fired — making a spectacular picture.

Left History in the making? Captain Snow with his new Assistant Secretary (Personnel), Second Officer Liz Nuttall, believed the first complement billet WRNS officer at sea.

Below On the occasion of the End of Commission Ball in Devonport on 9 December 1983, no fewer than seven ex-captains of **Hermes** managed to join Captain Snow. From left to right: Captain R C Dimmock, Rear Admiral D C Jenkin, Vice Admiral D R Reffell, Admiral Sir John Fieldhouse, Captain K A Snow, Admiral Sir William O'Brien, Rear Admiral R G A Fitch, and Rear Admiral L E Middleton.

Epilogue
The final days

Above Hermes (right) on her sea trials after her final refit sails past her 'half sister', **HMS Bulwark. Bulwark** was under tow bound for a Scottish scrapyard; April 1984. When will **Hermes** make the same journey?

Below Will she sail again? In summer 1984 **Hermes** lies in a quiet corner of Portsmouth Naval Base. A small ship's company carry out basic maintenance and, officially, she remains at 30 days' notice for sea.

154

Appendix

Nine forerunners   1796 to 1942

Above *Six Ospreys —* **Hermes'** *complete complement of this type of aircraft — lined up on the after deck* *with the carrier's Fairey Seals just visible to the left — note the RAF personnel.*

Ten ships bearing the proud name of *Hermes*, winged messenger of the gods, have served in the Royal Navy over a period of nearly two hundred years. The first ship so named was, however, captured in combat. This was the Dutch Brig *Mercurius*, rigged as a sloop and of 210 tons, with 14 guns. The English Fleet was blockading the Dutch coast, when men from Her Majesty's Ship *Sylph*, under Commander (later Vice Admiral Sir) John Chambers White boarded and captured her in 1796. As was the custom with a Navy desperate for ships at time of war, she was swiftly bought by the Royal Navy and renamed *Hermes*, another name for the god Mercury, and one which surmounted the problem of already having HMS *Mercury* in the Fleet. Sadly, though, the first *Hermes* was not destined for long and meritorious service, since she foundered, whilst under the command of Commander William Muslo, and was lost at sea with all hands in January 1797.

Their Lords of the Admiralty had seemingly become taken with the name, as the following year an armed vessel of 331 tons, carrying 80 men, was purchased for service on the North Sea Station and named *Hermes*. She was sold in 1802, but the name was perpetuated within a year again, when a sloop, built at Whitby and named *Majestic*, was purchased and renamed *Hermes*. Her career seems to have been a quiet one, but she saw service in the North Sea, the Channel, and South America. She finished her career as a storeship in the Mediterranean and was sold in 1810.

The fourth *Hermes* contributed greatly to the illustrious name of the ship. Built at HM Dockyard Portsmouth and launched on 22 July 1811, she spent the year of 1811–1812 serving in the North Sea and Channel stations; a 6th rate frigate of 512 tons, with 20 guns and a crew of 121 men. That year, under the command of Captain (later Vice Admiral) Philip Brown, the *Hermes* captured an American ship laden with naval stores and two vessels from New York and Baltimore carrying tobacco and ivory. The time was, of course, the American War of Independence. In September 1811 *Hermes* was responsible for running down the French privateer *La Mouche*. Captain Brown, a keen painter, recorded the action on canvas, which still hangs in the National Maritime Museum at Greenwich.

Captain Brown's service with the ship concluded with the capture of the American privateer *Sword Fish*, before command passed, in 1814, to Captain (later Rear Admiral) the Hon William Henry Percy. The ship then went to the Gulf of Mexico, in a force with three other ships and 200 soldiers, to attack Fort Bowyer at Mobile, Alabama, USA. On 12 September 1814 *Hermes* anchored off the fort, and on the 15th put a force ashore. The cable had to be cut during a counter-attack, and the ship drifted inshore and grounded. Disabled, her Captain ordered her to be burnt, to prevent her falling into enemy hands, and after losing twenty-five of her crew killed in action, and twenty-four wounded, the career of the fourth *Hermes* came to its end. . . .

There was then a period of sixteen years before the Navy had another ship named *Hermes*, and it was a far cry from its predecessor. She was a steam vessel of some 733 tons, built at Blackwall in 1824 and purchased by the Navy in 1830. The ex-*George IV* became the fifth *Hermes*, but only spent four years in the Packet Service, before being converted into a coal depot ship at Woolwich under the new name of *Charger*, and was broken up at Deptford in 1854. It is to be hoped that there was reasoning behind the change of name, as the new *Hermes*, a paddle-wheeled steam sloop of 830 tons, had a career in marked contrast to her predecessor.

Launched at Portsmouth Dockyard in 1835, the sixth *Hermes* served five years on the Mediterranean Station, followed by four years on the North American Station; she is particularly remembered, however, for

four exciting years' service which followed on the Cape of Good Hope and East Indies Station. Under the command of Commander Edmund G Fishbourne, the ship participated in the hostilities of 1851 against the Kaffirs, and 'rendered services to the value of which the strongest testimony was borne in the despatches of the Governor, Lieutenant General Sir Harry Smith'. The ship then sailed for the East Indies Station where, following illegal actions by the Burmese at Rangoon, contrary to an 1826 agreement, she joined a Task Force led by Commodore Lambert in HMS *Fox*, a 42-gun screw frigate. After negotiations ashore, conducted by Commander Fishbourne on behalf of the Commodore, all British subjects in Rangoon were evacuated and British merchantmen towed to safety. Rangoon was blockaded, and later *Hermes* participated in a combined naval and military assault on the Burmese town of Martaban, before assisting in the assault which captured Rangoon. The ship then went to the China Station, where she assisted in policing the seas against pirates and rebels. Commander Fishbourne had been promoted captain for his actions in Burma, but continued with the ship. After action-packed days either dealing with armed junks, venturing into rebel-held waters of the Yangtse, and escorting HM ambassadors, the ship returned home in 1854 to be paid off at Woolwich. After another five years' service, she was sold and broken up in 1864.

The seventh *Hermes* was launched at Chatham in 1816, and was originally named *Minotaur*. A 1,726-ton third rate, the renaming was on being taken up for service as a cholera hospital ship at Gravesend. She was broken up at Sheerness in 1869. It was a twenty-eight year period before the Navy commissioned the eighth *Hermes*. This was an eleven-gun, 477-man, protected cruiser of 5,600 tons. Laid down and launched on the Clyde in 1898, she entered naval service a year later.

During the next twelve years she saw service in many parts of the world, and for many purposes, and the picture overleaf shows one of the gunnery crews at drill in about 1906.

However, in 1913, she was fitted experimentally with sea plane launching rails on platforms over the fo'c's'le and quarterdeck, with the aircraft landing in the water on return – for recovery by crane. As such, she became the Royal Navy's first 'aircraft carrier', and took part in exercises with the fleet in July 1913, the first time aircraft had been used in conjunction with ships at sea. This launching equipment was removed in December 1913, when *Hermes* became the Depot ship for the Naval wing of the Royal Flying Corps. When war came in 1914, *Hermes* was again fitted to carry three sea planes. On completion of a mission ferrying aircraft to Dunkirk in October 1914, she was torpedoed by the German submarine U-27 off Calais. She sank with the loss of 23 lives.

In 1919 the honour of being the first vessel specifically designed as an aircraft carrier went to the ninth *Hermes*. Built by Armstrong Whitworth of Newcastle, she was launched on 11 September 1919, towed to Devonport and entered service in 1924. Displacing 10,950 tons, the ship was 598 feet long and was capable of a speed of 25 knots from two shaft geared turbines developing 40,000 shp. Protected by armour, she was armed with 6 x 5.5-inch guns, 3 x 4-inch AA guns and 18 machine guns manned by Royal Marines. She carried a crew of 664. Originally she carried 21 aircraft, but as they became larger, so the number embarked shrank, until by the Second World War she carried only 12 Swordfish aircraft. The squadron nevertheless became familiar, as it was 814 Naval Air Squadron, who continued their association with the ship in action from these early days until the Falklands campaign.

The ninth *Hermes* was recorded as being a comfortable ship at sea, possibly for her time the most stable ship in the Navy. First because she sat well down in the water and, secondly, to provide the necessary width of her flight deck (90 feet), her hull was given a considerable flare outwards and upwards at her bows — and this was carried aft for about 200 feet. The net result was that she did not roll much, and her pitching movement was heavily dampened by the flare at the bows. This also necessitated low positions for the anchors and, together with the heavy tripod mast supporting the range finders and control top, made her easily identifiable.

Though much of the ship's service pre-war is recorded as being with the Home Fleet, it was the custom to undertake two short cruises and one long one each year to 'show the flag'. This explains why the ninth *Hermes* spent so much time on the China Station and, in particular, became such a well-known sight at the Fleet anchorage of Wai Hai Wei in China. At this time, a squadron of Seals (824 NAS) and a squadron of Ospreys were embarked, and included many RAF air and ground crews. As at the present time, the mysteries of naval tradition were explained — as one RAF officer recalled when leaning on the guard rails of the quarterdeck shortly after anchoring... 'I was absorbed in the fascination of all the new sights and sounds around us, when the quiet but pained voice of the Officer of the Watch said over my left shoulder "Don't lean on the guardrail, old chap. This is the Navy, not the P&O".'...

The start of the Second World War found *Hermes* patrolling her war station at Portland, part of the Channel Force with HMS *Courageous*. She was transferred to the West Indies Station and helped counter the threat of the *Graf Spee*. She then moved to the South Atlantic and joined with the French battlecruiser *Strasbourg* to form a raider hunting group, operating from Dakar in French West Africa. With the French capitulation in 1940, the captain of the *Hermes* was forced to take his ship to sea from what had been a friendly port. At sea the ship received the news that her Captain had been promoted Temporary Rear Admiral and was to deliver an ultimatum to the French Admiral at Dakar to surrender, with all his ships and men, or force was to be used. *Hermes* had with her the cruisers *Dorsetshire* and *Australia*, but in Dakar was the brand new battleship *Richelieu*, as well as heavily fortified gun batteries and other hostile forces.

The ultimatum was rejected by the French, and worse still, having only just finished sharing a hangar ashore with the French, the next experience of 814 NAS was to suffer a bombing attack on the ship — from their previous hosts! The ship's response was to launch a combined air and sneak attack at dawn on 7 July 1940, by Swordfish aircraft carrying torpedoes and the ship's power boat carrying depth charges. The boat attack was successful, with four depth charges being laid under the stern of the *Richelieu*, and at least two torpedoes striking the battleship. The boat, and all six aircraft, were safely recovered, together with their crews.

After this action, *Hermes* returned to Freetown and was employed on anti-submarine patrols and convoy duties off East Africa. Unfortunately, late in 1941 she collided with the armed merchant cruiser *Corfu* on one such convoy. With the bows stove in, and the flight deck torn off forrard and flattened on to the cable deck, she limped into Simonstown for repair in December 1941.

It was, sadly, to prove the ship's last Christmas as, repaired by March 1942, she left to join the Eastern Fleet at Colombo. On 8 March 1942 *Hermes*, in company with HMAS *Vampire*, was ordered to sail from Trincomalee, in order to avoid anticipated Japanese air attacks. Unfortunately, she was spotted by a Japanese reconnaisance aircraft and was attacked by a force of some fifty aircraft. The ship did not stand a chance, armed with its few World War One AA guns, plus a few Oerlikons. Hit by some 40 bombs in little over ten minutes, she was sunk off Batticaloa, Ceylon. Her Commanding Officer, the much-loved Captain R F J Onslow, 18 other officers and 268 ratings were lost, together with HMAS *Vampire*, the corvette *Hollyhock*, and two tankers. A nearby hospital ship picked up 600 survivors from the tragedy.

HMS Hermes
Burma War 1852

1898

HERMES

HMBrig HERMES
1796

158

Above 8th **Hermes** — *gunnery crew at drill, circa 1906.*

Right *Torpedoed by U27 30 October 1914 in the Dover Straits, while returning from Dunkirk.*

Facing *Four famous predecessors*

HMS HERMES

Her Commanding Officers

23 October 1959 – 29 September 1961	Captain D S Tibbets DSC RN
30 September 1961 – 23 November 1961	Commander L McArdle MVO GM RN
24 November 1961 – 5 March 1964	Captain W D O'Brien DSC RN
6 March 1964 – 7 January 1965	Commander D J Bent DSC RN
8 January 1965 – 2 February 1966	Commander G T Riordon RN
3 February 1966 – 22 October 1967	Captain T T Lewin MVO DSC RN
23 October 1967 – 8 December 1967	Captain D G Parker DSO DSC AFC RN
9 December 1967 – 20 January 1968	Captain J D Fieldhouse RN
21 January 1968 – 1 July 1969	Captain D G Parker DSO DSC AFC RN
2 July 1969 – 3 September 1970	Captain P M Austin RN
4 September 1970 – 9 October 1970	Commander J B Rumble RN
10 October 1970 – 11 October 1970	Commander A W Wheeler RN
12 October 1970 – 16 November 1972	Commander H G Vere RN
17 November 1972 – 26 February 1973	Commander A D Hutton RN
27 February 1973 – 8 November 1974	Captain C R P C Branson RN
9 November 1974 – 27 May 1976	Captain D R Reffell RN
28 May 1976 – 20 September 1976	Commander P J Erskine RN
21 September 1976 – 21 April 1978	Captain R G A Fitch RN
22 April 1978 – 9 December 1979	Captain D C Jenkin RN
10 December 1979 – 3 November 1980	Captain D J MacKenzie RN
4 November 1980 – 19 September 1982	Captain L E Middleton RN
20 September 1982 – 22 August 1983	Captain R C Dimmock RN
23 August 1983 – 11 May 1984	Captain K A Snow RN
12 May 1984 –	Commander J A Bolger RN

Acknowledgements

One of the many Navy photographers whose work appears throughout this book

An account as brief as this can, of course, only scratch the surface, covering as it does 25 years in the life of the tenth HMS *Hermes*, and 188 years of the ten *Hermes*'s service in the Royal Navy.

I must therefore apologise for all those significant events which I have either missed, or have not covered in the depth some of my readers would undoubtedly have wished to see.

However, I have tried to spread stories and coverage below decks and in other departments, as well as the air operations which are the prime function of the carrier. In this I have been enormously helped and would wish to acknowledge my debt to all those who laboured to produce previous commissioning books, from which I have drawn unashamedly.

In addition, considerable assistance has been given by all those ex-*Hermes* personnel who have both written and lent photographs from personal collections. In particular, the following deserve mention: Ms Mary Butcher, Commander H K Dean OBE RN (Retd), Colonel D J Brewster MC RM (Retd), Mrs E Hartshorn, J R Smith, CY T Wargent RNR, R T Sinfield, D Swetnam, L/ Steward Cooper, Lt Glyn Davies RN, Commander P J Perraton RN, Commander A K Tatman RN, Lt C F Motley RN (Retd), R Smith, Captain P S Jones RN (Retd), Captain I Campbell RN (Retd), T W West, T Bryant, P Catchlove and Lieutenant Commander R Nicholl RN, and the many naval photographers whose handiwork will doubtless be admired by all those who read this book.

My thanks are also due to the publishers of *Flight Deck* magazine, and to the Fleet Air Arm Museum at NAS Yeovilton, *The News*, Portsmouth, the Associated Press Bureau, the Fleet Photographic Unit at Hilsea, and the Captain's Office staff of HMS *Hermes*.

Especially my gratitude goes to my Captain, now Rear Admiral Ken Snow, and to Mike Critchley of Maritime Books, for their encouragement and assistance, to Lord Lewin for writing the foreword, and last, but by no means least, to my wife Sheila for all her hard work and sacrifices on the book's behalf!